MW00713407

*HOW TO HAVE INTERCOURSE
WITHOUT GETTING SCREWED*

How to Have Intercourse Without Getting Screwed

JENNIFER WEAR and KING HOLMES

Madrona Publishers, Inc. • *Seattle*

Library of Congress Cataloging in Publication Data

Wear, Jennifer, 1947–
    How to have intercourse without getting screwed.

    1. Conception--Prevention.   2. Abortion.
3. Venereal diseases.   4. Sexual intercourse.
I. Holmes, King, 1937–   joint author.   II. Ti-
tle.
RG136.W37   613.9   76–41190
ISBN 0–914842–12–9 pbk.

Madrona Publishers, Inc.
113 Madrona Place East
Seattle, Washington 98112

PREFACE

There have been guides written to tell you how, when, why, and whether to have sex. This is not a guide but a rule book, our attempt to put down some rules about having sex. The rules aren't our own arbitrary inventions: they are defined by natural law and evolution. And since compliance with the rules is almost completely voluntary, we've also tried to explain the penalties for breaking the rules.

Life is full of rules designed to protect you and your fellow humans from hurting each other, and you can't avoid being taught rules about every important social interaction except one. Before you can drive a car, you have to learn the rules of the road and pass a licensing exam. Even boxers learn the Marquis of Queensbury rules. At your job you may be required to wear a hard hat, a lab coat, safety glasses, or a parachute. Even in the delicate matters of personal hygiene you learn the rules almost as soon as you acquire your vocabulary: "Cover your mouth when you cough! Use your handkerchief—don't sneeze on the baby! Did you wipe? I didn't see any paper in the bowl! Wash your hands before you come to the table!"

When it comes to sex there are no licensing exams. Anyone

can play, whether he or she knows what he or she is doing. Any attempt to teach young people how to avoid unwanted pregnancy or sexually transmitted diseases is often misconstrued as an attempt to promote promiscuous sexual behavior. Where a genuine attempt is made to provide such information, it is often made by someone who doesn't have the information—a misinformed parent or an inadequately prepared teacher, perhaps. The family physician is not likely to know some of the essential information, particularly the latest information about sexually transmitted diseases. And even if the health care professionals had all this information, they couldn't possibly give in an office visit the information you need to have to make responsible and educated decisions in sexual matters.

This book contains the latest accurate information on contraception, abortion, and sexually transmitted diseases. It is written for people who believe ignorance can be self-destructive, and want hard information that is not sugar-coated. It is for people who are sexually active or who think they might like to become sexually active some day—in or out of love, in or out of marriage, with or without children.

We hope accurate information will remove some of the myths, fears, and irrational anxieties surrounding sexuality, and we hope it will help people behave more responsibly in their relationships.

ACKNOWLEDGMENTS

In 1970 the Associated Students of the University of Washington (ASUW) Women's Commission published a booklet with the title *How to Have Intercourse . . . without Getting Screwed*. The authors of that booklet, Barbara Reskin, Lynn Hansen, and Diana Grey, filled a great need for health care information at the University. Subsequently, while working on my undergraduate degree in zoology, I rewrote and updated the second edition of that booklet, which was published in 1975.

This book began as an attempt to expand and update the earlier editions of the booklet and make it available to a wider public. But it quickly became apparent that the great amount of material available, the great number of unanswered questions, and, most importantly, the public's desire for much more information than had previously been offered called for a completely new work.

While we have kept nothing of the original booklet except the title—and that with the hope of reaching the widest possible audience—this book would not have been possible without the initiative and dedication of Barbara Reskin, Lynn

Hansen, and Diana Grey, the ASUW Women's Commission, and Dr. Elaine Henley.

One day, while I was doing research on sexually transmitted diseases in Dr. King Holmes' library, Dr. Holmes came by and asked me what I was doing. I told him I was writing a book, what the book was about, and what it was called. He told me he had a secret literary fantasy to write a book about sexually transmitted diseases for the public, and he offered to collaborate with me. Obviously, Dr. Holmes was the best qualified person to write that part of the book. That is how he became the co-author.

There have been many people in and out of the medical community who have generously given me their advice and counsel. I would like to extend my appreciation to Cornelius Rosse, professor of biological structure at the University of Washington School of Medicine, for his short course on reproductive anatomy; to Julian Ansell, professor and chairman of the Department of Urology at the University of Washington School of Medicine, who practically co-authored the section on oral contraceptives; Ruth Krauss, M.D., obstetrician and gynecologist at Group Health Cooperative and former medical director of Planned Parenthood Center of Seattle, who gave me permission to update her pamphlet on menopause and contraception and reviewed my final draft; Russ DeJong, M.D., obstetrician and gynecologist of Harborview Women's Clinic, for his help on several contraceptive sections and for providing me with many review articles; Helen K. Kolbe, Project Director, Population Reports, George Washington University Population Information Program, Washington, D.C., for providing me with all the current bulletins on contraception and abortion which were invaluable; Aimee Bakken, professor of zoology at the University of Washington, for her guidance and support; Markham Harris, professor of english at the University of Washington, who was keenly aware that the style in which this book was written was the right one; Frans Koome, M.D., who initiated the first Reproductive Crisis Clinic in Seattle and who reviewed every choice of word and tone of the abortion section—his thoughts and feelings on abortion have developed through much experience and consideration for the impact of unwanted pregnancies on human beings; Barbara Schneidman, M.D., M.P.H., co-director of Gynecorps, and Julie Schneidmiller and Jean Brickell, women's health care specialists, who read and commented on all parts of the book which I authored. A special note of thanks to Ellie Kauffman, third-year medical student at the University of Washington School of Medicine, confidante— whose encouragement, support, and wisdom have been invaluable; and another to Gordon White who encouraged me to write this book and who had the confidence that I could do it.

Finally, both King and I are grateful for the guidance and endurance of our publisher, Dan Levant, who unfailingly reminded us to keep the textbook language on the shelf and out of this book.

JENNIFER WEAR

I am gratefully indebted to each and everyone of the sexually transmitted diseases for making my investigative career so interesting, and to my esteemed colleagues whose research findings are detailed herein.

KING HOLMES

CONTENTS

*HOW TO HAVE INTERCOURSE
WITHOUT GETTING SCREWED*

JUST ENOUGH ANATOMY

The human body is an incredibly sturdy machine, but it needs some care and attention. And those parts of the body which are committed to reproduction are particularly vulnerable in certain ways. The trouble is that most people know more about the parts of their car than the parts of their body.

Under cover of the skin, the processes of sex go on all the time: sex cells are being made, stimulated to grow by hormones, transported from one place to another—all towards that goal of fertilization and reproduction of the species. From time to time, throbbing genitals get together and make it happen. But most sexual acts are not intended to reproduce the species. They happen because they make people feel good, because they offer comfort, warmth, closeness, an emotional high, relief, distraction, all sorts of things that have nothing to do with fertilization. Many people find heterosexual intercourse the ultimate high, the ultimate interaction. Most of the time they don't want fertilization; it would be an unwanted side effect. But since the whole system is working towards that end, it takes positive action to interrupt it, it takes active intervention to see that it doesn't happen. And it takes knowledge to be able to intervene sensibly and re-liably.

Sexually transmitted diseases (a much better term than "venereal") are certainly an unwanted side effect, but some of them have reached the status of full-scale epidemics. About 3,000,000 cases of gonorrhea occurred in the United States in 1975. Active intervention can offer protection against getting a sexually transmitted disease. It certainly is called for if you have one and are going to get proper and early treatment. That takes knowledge, too, and an awareness of how the body works.

Understanding and relating to our bodies is protection, like buying insurance. It's exciting, like finding out how any-thing works. It's an obligation, learning how to take care of our most valuable possession. We make incredible demands on it, many times give it poor care, don't have the slightest idea how it works, and feel betrayed if something goes wrong. Then, if we come up against a physician or some other health-care person who keeps us in the dark, we feel helpless in our ignorance.

We don't have to be physicians or other medical profession-als to learn the names, locations, and functions of our sex organs and the hormones which run the show. Taking the time to learn the basic health language pays off right now; it makes us better consumers of health care, results in better decisions about contraception, and protects us from the things we don't want to happen when we use those organs. This is the most basic body language.

WOMEN'S BODIES

Women's bodies are great. Maybe the greatest thing they can do is make another human being. But most of the time they aren't making babies and they're great anyway. Few

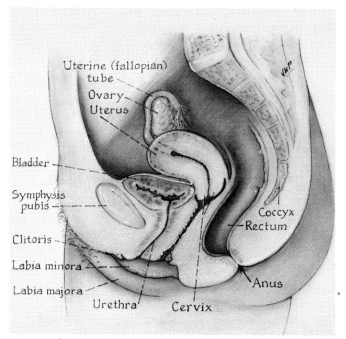

women, however, know very much about their sex organs and genitals, in part due to the fact that most of these are hidden from view and in part because we are not encouraged to explore. Until the tampon was introduced, we rarely felt our genitals. And putting our fingers into our vaginas was a real no-no. We don't need to hold anything while urinating and our sexual response does not have such an obvious signpost as an erect penis.

We got a lot of nonverbal signals (men got them, too) from other people, like our parents, in respect to fooling around with our genitals or asking questions about our sexual parts. There is no other area in life that is quite as uncomfortable for most people to talk about as sex, especially to our children. So this uncomfortable feeling is passed on from generation to generation and now we are attempting to overcome the emotional overtones and stigmas attached to our own sexuality and to learn how our bodies work.

Most women have never seen their clitoris (klit-or-iss). Can you imagine a boy growing up and when he is an adult, telling him you are now going to show him where his penis is? True, the clitoris is not as obvious and we need to look for it but it brings the same amount of pleasure. Knowing we have an organ whose sole function is to give us pleasure is nice and is great for our self-esteem.

Looking at our genitals, touching our genitals, literally finding our sexual parts is difficult for most women. We have grown up without looking, without touching, and indeed without finding our sexual parts. Our genital area, our sexuality, is emotionally charged. It is difficult to forget all the social cues we've known, to cast off our inhibitions and pretend it is easy; it's not easy. We all have to make an effort, but it's possible.

The best way to go about this is to look at yourself in front of a mirror—here's the tough part—without your clothes on. Step one, turn up the heat. Then, you can pull up a chair to a full-length mirror and sit down, or even better, use a hand mirror (compact mirror is a bit small) and sit on a chair, bed, or the floor—wherever you're comfortable. Place the mirror in front of your genitals and look at yourself. We're all pretty used to looking at our pubic hair arranged in a triangular pattern over the pubic bone but we're not used to looking at all the parts between our legs. The most obvious feature is two folds of skin covered with pubic hair which are next to the inside of the legs. Before the growth of our genitals at puberty, these folds are hairless and are about all that are noticeable in a young girl. They are called the labia majora. Now prop the mirror so as to free your hands. Press these folds of skin toward your legs as the other parts are described. Directly below the pubic bone, where the two folds begin to form a crease, you'll find the clitoris. It is very sensitive to the touch because it has many nerve endings for sexual sensation. If you put your finger on top of it, it will feel like a small mound about the size of a pea. You can feel the stem of the clitoris by pressing with two fingers on either side of this mound. It is about an inch long altogether but you won't be able to feel its base.

When a woman becomes sexually excited this organ fills with blood and becomes erect just as a man's penis becomes filled with blood and hence erect when he is excited. Since this sex part is difficult to see, there are some other ways you can locate it. At the place where the inner lips, or labia minora, meet is the clitoris. In fact, the junction of these inner folds of skin forms a hood over the clitoris. The clitoris lies directly above where urine flows out of your body.

Below the clitoris lies the urethral opening, then the vaginal opening below that, and finally the anal opening. Because these openings are so close together, it is very easy for bacteria to be displaced into the wrong opening which can result in irritation or infection. The design engineer for this area of a woman's body should have been fired.

The inner lips, or labia minora, run parallel to the labia majora, fold together, and cover the urethral as well as the vaginal openings. They are not covered by pubic hair and are more delicate since they don't have the same tough covering of skin as do the outer folds of skin. There are glands on the inside of these folds of skin. You won't be able to see them but you can know about where they are and what they do. A gland is a part of the body or organ which has a special function: it secretes fluid. These glands secrete a thick liquid particularly when a woman becomes sexually aroused.

Urine passes from the bladder to the outside through a channel called the urethra. Because the opening of this channel is difficult to see, put your finger into your vagina (as if you were inserting a tampon) and push downward. Just above the vagina, the opening of the urethra will appear from between the inner folds. It is a slightly raised area of tissue that is shaped like an upside-down V.

Now for the vagina. The vagina is a muscular channel that connects the uterus to the outside. It envelops the penis during intercourse, and during childbirth it is capable of tremendous expansion so the baby can pass to the outside. Although the vagina is a channel, its walls press together when they aren't being pushed apart. The outer one-third of the vagina has many nerve endings, unlike the inner portion of the vagina. The inner portion, though, is sensitive to pressure. In most newborn girls there is a hymen just inside the opening of the vagina. The hymen is a thin membrane containing blood vessels and with a woman's first intercourse this membrane will tear, causing blood to flow. It is important to note that the size and thickness of the hymen vary greatly, depending on the individual, and some baby girls are born without one. In addition, general physical activity such as riding bicycles or horses can cause the hymen to tear. Throughout history the intact hymen has been the sign of purity for women. In some cultures, it was necessary for the hymen to be intact for marriage. Obviously, for the females who were born without a hymen or for those whose hymen was torn through accident, the consequences were severe. We are fortunate our society is not very worried about the intact hymen.

Now that we know something about our external sexual parts, what about our internal organs? What we know about ourselves including our genitals which we have just looked at is usually in two dimensions, not three dimensions. Pictures we see of ourselves are in two dimensions and pictures of bodies in books are in two dimensions—but we are real and not textbook pages. So we are unaccustomed to knowing what things that we can't see (like our internal sexual organs) look like—not only from the front, but from the side, and from the back. And we are unaccustomed to knowing their relationship to other organs and structures.

Let's make a jump and try to think of ourselves in three dimensions. Standing in front of a full-length mirror will help.

Imagine that you took a string and wrapped it around your body so it touched your navel in front and was slightly above the crease that your buttocks make in the back. From this circle to where your legs join your body is where all the parts of the female reproductive system can be found within you. You can find the uterus, uterine tubes, ovaries, and the muscular wall of the vagina in this area. (The bladder and urethra are also there but are not a part of reproduction.) Looking within from the front, the first things you see are your intestines and pubic bone. Then, setting them aside, you see the largest part of the uterus bending toward you as it hunches over the bladder. To understand the 3-D relationship of these organs plus the vagina, opening of the uterus (termed "cervix"), uterine tubes, and ovaries, make a fist. Your fist represents the uterus; your wrist represents the most narrow portion of the uterus, or cervix; and your forearm is like the muscular wall of the vagina. Now bend your wrist forward. Normally the uterus bends forward like this, tipping in the direction of the navel. The uterus is a muscular structure about the size of a small fist in a woman who has not had any children. It remains slightly expanded after pregnancy, but if a woman is larger after pregnancy it is not due to the increase in the size of the uterus but to overeating.

The uterus is where the menstrual flow or "period" originates. It is also the site of the development of a baby. Sperm must pass through the uterus to the tubes for fertilization to occur. To aid the passage of sperm, there is a hormone which causes the uterus to contract. Intercourse will cause release of this hormone and result in this muscular action. Without this aid, sperm would never reach the site of fertilization as quickly as they do (about 30 minutes).

The female bladder lies underneath the tipped portion of the uterus. The bladder is a hollow organ with muscular walls that expand when filled with urine. Pregnant women urinate often because of pressure on the bladder caused by the growing fetus inside the uterus.

Next, imagine there are tubes coming out either side of your closed fist or "uterus." These are the uterine tubes. These two tubes extend from either side of the upper surface of the uterus and outward in the direction of the hip bones. They are several inches long (10 to 12 centimeters) and logically called the uterine tubes. (The old-fashioned name is Fallopian tube.) Each tube has a fringe-like end which caresses an ovary. These tubes carry the eggs (ova) from the ovaries, and sperm from the uterus into the tubes. The site of fertilization is in these tubes. They are very complex and the inner surfaces are covered with tiny hair-like structures called cilia. These beat constantly to move the ovum toward the uterus.

The ovaries have a beginning similar to the testicles in a man. One of the major differences between the development of the ovaries and the testicles is that the testes (having developed inside the main body cavity) move down through the body in about the seventh month of prenatal development and come into position outside the main body cavity within the scrotal sac. When a woman is born, there are about 400,000 eggs in both her ovaries. Obviously, not all of these ova are released by the ovaries, but any one of them can be "chosen" to develop and be subsequently released. An ovum breaks through the wall of the ovary about every 30 days and is captured by the fringe-like end of the uterine tube. The ovum travels along the uterine tube, and if sperm are present, one penetrates the egg. What's really neat is that only one sperm can enter an egg even though there are many sperm present. After penetration of the ovum by one sperm, the surface of the ovum changes so no more sperm can enter.

In addition to producing eggs the ovaries produce female and male hormones just like the testicles but there are more female hormones than male hormones produced in a woman.

Female Orgasm

In women, the organ of sexual pleasure—the clitoris— is distinct from the organs of reproduction. The vagina, although it reacts to sexual stimulation, has few nerve endings for sex sensation and the role that penetration plays in orgasm is almost entirely psychological. Generally, orgasm is the result of direct or indirect stimulation of the clitoris, which has lots of nerve endings for sex sensation. This stimulation may occur directly by gentle touching with your fingers or your partner's fingers or tongue, or indirectly by body contact during intercourse. When a woman is having intercourse the man's pubic bone is pressing against and rubbing her genital area above her vagina, and this is enough stimulation to bring some women to orgasm. Other women cannot have an orgasm with this indirect stimulation. That does not mean there is anything wrong with them. A woman's sexual response is often more complicated than a man's response and requires her knowing her body and what interaction is necessary to bring about sexual satisfaction.

Men are sometimes unaware of this organ of excitement or not sure where to find it. So a woman might tell her partner what feels good to her. Many times our inhibitions about sexuality in general prevent us from communicating with our sexual partners. If a woman has difficulty saying the exact words, she can place her partner's fingers on her clitoris and ask him to gently rub her in this area. From a man's point of view, this is similar to having the tip of his penis massaged and, as in the male, direct firm rubbing of this area results in irritation and is very uncomfortable. One of the nicest aids in stimulation of the clitoris is to use some kind of lubricant; there is less friction on the sensitive area and the lubrication decreases soreness from prolonged stimulation. It is very possible to have an orgasm without having intercourse, by massaging this area. Oral stimulation is very pleasant to many women due to the delicate touch of the tongue and the lubrication of saliva.

It is important to point out that achieving an orgasm is not a goal a woman has to set for herself every time she has intercourse. Sexual response will vary according to your mood, how much energy you have, how you feel towards your sexual partner, and your attitude toward any other way in which you stimulate yourself, whether it be by sexual fantasy, masturbation, or the use of a vibrator. If, for example, a woman has always felt uncomfortable about masturbation, it is doubtful she will achieve the greatest pleasure through this kind of stimulation. The important question is, "Are your sexual experiences rewarding and satisfying?"

Pelvic Floor Muscles—Exercises

The muscles a woman uses to stop the flow of urine and to tighten the rectum also surround her vagina and give support to her uterus and bladder. They are known collectively as the pelvic floor muscles. After childbirth these muscles are stretched and lack tone unless properly exercised; as we grow older, particularly with poor posture and overeating, these muscles relax, and this may cause urinary problems.

If you put your finger into either the opening of the vagina or the rectum during orgasm, you would feel the rhythmic tightening of the pelvic floor muscles around your finger. When these muscles lack tone or are not strong, a downward force such as a sneeze or a cough can result in spontaneous loss of urine called urinary incontinence. Some specific exercises for the pelvic floor muscles were designed originally by Dr. Arnold Kegel to help women hold urine when they sneezed or coughed. The exercises are also recommended after childbirth since the pelvic floor muscles are stretched tremendously when the baby comes through the vagina. And they can be done by any woman at any age to tighten and have more control over her vagina during intercourse. What both partners will find particularly nice is the tightening of these muscles each time the penis is withdrawn from the vagina or the vagina is withdrawn from the penis.

Slackness in the pelvic floor can be made worse by poor posture, overweight, and lack of exercise in general. If a woman is in the habit of standing with her abdomen pushed forward and the pelvic muscles relaxed, she is contributing to the lack of tone in this area.

One practical thing about these exercises is that they can be done anytime and anywhere without anyone else knowing—while riding to work, reading, and so on.

To become familiar with these muscles, tighten the rectum just as you would during a bowel movement. This tightening will also stop the flow of urine, but it's not a good idea to do these exercises while urinating. If the thigh, stomach, or buttock muscles are tightening, the pelvic floor muscles are not being exercised. Now, the exercises:

1) Squeeze and lift the pelvic floor muscles for three sec-

onds, then relax for three seconds. Then again, squeeze and lift for three seconds, then relax for the same amount of time. At the beginning, repeat this sequence ten times at three different times during the day. A woman might discover at first that squeezing these muscles for three seconds is difficult so she can begin by squeezing for one or two seconds until the muscles are strengthened.

2) Another exercise consists of imagining the muscles are pulling a tampon into your vagina. Do this for three or more seconds. This will give you an idea of the lifting motion emphasized in the first exercise. This lift concept is extremely important in exercising the muscles around the base of the bladder. In addition, control of the entire length of the vagina during intercourse is pleasurable to both the woman and the man, particularly while the man gradually withdraws his penis.

3) Finally, imagine you are pushing a tampon out of the vagina and hold this for three seconds as well. This exercise can be alternated with the one above. They can all be done ten times each at three different times during the day. Of course if a woman has any soreness she can do each five times instead of ten.

MEN'S BODIES

Whereas women's sexual organs are hidden inside the main body cavity, men have had their testicles and penis in full view since they were born. But there are lots of other parts of the male reproductive system that most men don't know about. For example, the prostate gland, which will cause many men difficulty as they grow older, is part of the system, and without knowledge of the position and function of it men find themselves unprepared for this problem.

In contrast to women, men have been accustomed not only to touching their genitals but to being praised for doing so

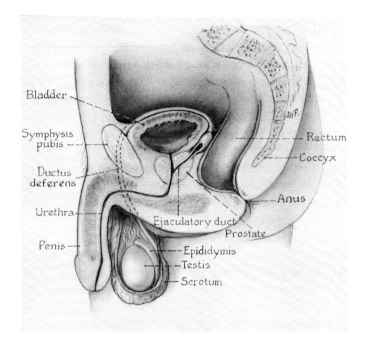

Bladder

Symphysis
pubis

Ductus
deferens

Urethra

Penis

Ejaculatory duct

Prostate

Epididymis

Testis

Scrotum

Rectum

Coccyx

Anus

while urinating. If there were a way around genital touching, no doubt it would have been implemented before now. So while getting used to urinating, a boy also gets used to relating to his genitals physically and psychologically.

Men are continuously producing sperm in their testicles, unlike females who are born with all the ova they will need for a lifetime. In order for sperm manufacture to occur, the testicles must be at a considerably lower temperature than normal body temperature, and the testicles are conveniently located outside the main body cavity for this reason. What is fascinating is that it takes approximately two and one-half months to make one sperm. Only a dozen or so actually reach the site of fertilization in the uterine tube of the female.

There are two testicles. Each one has a separate channel leading from it that runs through the groin and into the back of the prostate gland. After entering the back of the prostate, these channels feed into the urethra which runs through the middle of the prostate gland.

Tracing sperm from their origin to where they end up is an interesting journey and all the male reproductive organs and structures can be pointed out along the way. Since both pathways are the same we can follow just one pathway, remembering that there are two of each structure mentioned until we get to the urethra.

The sperm leave the testicle and travel through a tightly coiled tube called the epididymis. The sperm which enter the epididymis are not able to fertilize an egg; they need to go through a maturing process in the epididymis. In addition, this area stores sperm. At this point the sperm are still inside tubes in the scrotum.

Immediately after the epididymis is the vas deferens. It can be thought of as a continuation of the epididymis but it has a different name because it is straight and not coiled and it doesn't store or mature sperm as the epididymis does. Shortly after we reach the vas deferens we are in the main body cavity. The vas deferens is the tube which is cut and sealed off during a vasectomy. As you can see, since sperm is the only thing that travels through each vas deferens, sperm will be the only part missing from an ejaculation after a vasectomy. And since sperm make up such a very small part of the total volume of each ejaculation, the difference is not noticeable. If you were to place 150 to 500 million sperm (the number in one ejaculation) in a pile, the mass would be about the same as a shirt button!

The sperm then flow through the remainder of the vas deferens and reach the enlarged portion of the vas deferens called the ampulla. The ampulla then narrows, forming the ejaculatory duct which pierces the back of the prostate.

The seminal vesicle is directly below the ampulla or expanded portion of the vas deferens and is connected to the vas deferens just before it enters the back of the prostate. The seminal vesicle is a gland which makes and secretes fluid. The fluids from the seminal vesicle also feed into the ejaculatory duct, mixing with sperm from the ampullar portion of the vas. These fluids make up the major part of the semen (seminal fluid). Both the seminal vesicle and prostate gland are unaffected by a vasectomy, and consequently ejaculation will be the same as before the operation.

When ejaculation occurs, both ejaculatory ducts empty into the urethra, the prostate gland contributes its fluids, and the mixture is forced out the urethra by muscular contractions. Although ejaculation is a specific happening, secretions can escape earlier from the tip of the penis without the male being aware of it. The first moisture at the tip of the penis upon sexual stimulation is in the form of a crystal-clear fluid from the bulbo-urethral glands, pea-sized pouches attached to the urethra. Their secretions may contain live sperm which cause pregnancy. For this reason withdrawal, also called coitus interruptus, is not an effective method of contraception.

It is interesting to know that if the base of the bladder were not shut tightly during ejaculation most of the semen would not come out the end of the penis but would be forced into the bladder. Nature put a circular muscle around the opening to the bladder and this muscle closes tightly during ejaculation. This muscle normally serves to hold urine in the bladder. Contrary to popular belief, urination with an erection is possible but there has to be a little more effort due to the fact that the urine is going uphill.

In many areas of life the emphasis has been on quantity rather than quality and the male genitals have not escaped this value system. Consequently there is great anxiety about the size of the male genitals, as there has been about the size of the female breasts. What needs to be emphasized is that there is a wide range of what's normal, that the size of the penis before an erection does not indicate the size of an erect penis, and that the vagina is only three to four inches long. Ultimately, it is not how big the penis is but what a man does with it that's important. Masturbation will not increase the size of the penis.

Masturbation is normal. About 97 percent of all teen-age boys masturbate as does the majority of the adult male population. Regardless of society's attitudes people will continue to masturbate just because it feels good. This is a normal event in the teen-age discovery of sexual awareness and ability and has nothing to do with an unhealthy mind or body. It can also be a sexual alternative for males and females after puberty if they are not comfortable with an intimate relationship or if contraceptives are not available to them. Even if a male masturbates frequently he will not run out of semen. The prostate gland and seminal vesicle will merely increase production.

Most men experience urinary problems as they grow older due to abnormal growths in the prostate gland. The most common abnormal growth or tumor is called benign nodular hyperplasia of the prostate. This disease begins to appear in men at about the age of 45 and 80 percent of the male population which has reached 80 years of age is affected more or less with obstruction of the bladder neck which makes urination difficult. This problem is not the result of sexual activity nor is it hereditary.

If you understand that the prostate gland surrounds the

urethra at the base of the bladder then you can see how enlargement of the prostate would cause difficulty with urination to a greater or lesser degree. The location of these tumors or nodules has a lot to do with the amount of obstruction they cause and if obstruction is severe the nodules are removed surgically.

The early symptoms of prostate trouble are slight hesitation at the beginning of urination, decrease in the diameter of the stream, increased frequency of urination during the day and evening, and interruption of urination. These symptoms, though, can be mild and unchanging for months or years.

Circumcision is the most common operation on male infants in the United States. The medical necessity for this procedure has not been established, although there is evidence that circumcised men are less susceptible to certain sexually-transmitted diseases. In the Jewish religion it is a mark of cleanliness. An uncircumcised male may have more problems with inflammation and infection, and he needs to keep the area underneath the foreskin clean by daily washing with mild soap and water. There are glands in the foreskin of the penis which secrete a thick liquid called smegma. This liquid has a foul odor and can collect in the pocket that the foreskin makes with the tip of the penis. Not all glands are removed when a baby is circumcised, but there is no pocket in which these fluids can collect.

HORMONES

You can't talk about sex without talking about hormones. Hormones direct the development of a fetus into a female or a male. Hormones regulate our growth, development, and normal body functions from infancy through puberty and all the way to the end. Breasts, beards, pubic hair, erections, menstruation, fertility—all things having to do with our sexuality—are affected, regulated, controlled, or somehow involved with hormones.

Everybody has been hearing a lot about hormones lately, particularly in relation to oral contraceptives. But hormones are rarely defined or described, and their role in normal body functioning does not make the press—only the adverse effects of artificial hormones have been considered noteworthy.

There are things about hormones that are nice to know; there are other things you really ought to know. You can't make a sensible decision about oral contraceptives, for example, or deal with the body changes that result from taking them, without knowing something about how natural hormones affect our bodies.

Hormones are chemical messengers which are produced by glands in various parts of the body. These messengers are carried by the bloodstream to other parts of the body. To stimulate reproduction the pituitary gland, which is located in the brain, produces hormones which travel through the bloodstream to signal the ovaries or the testicles. In the male these hormone messengers trigger the production of sperm and the production of the male hormone testosterone. In the female these hormone messengers begin the development of an egg, or ovum, and, in turn, the tissues around the growing ovum produce the female hormone estrogen. The ovaries and the testicles both produce male and female hormones, but the female produces more estrogen and the male produces more testosterone.

Although hormones are being made and are traveling in our bodies all our lives, puberty marks a time when specific hormones from the pituitary gland are "turned on." These hormones in turn trigger the increased production of other hormones in the testicles and ovaries. Boys suddenly experience erections and ejaculations.

Their hormones also signal the growth of the genitals and are responsible for pubic, underarm, and, finally, facial hair. In girls, sex hormones produced at puberty in the ovaries trigger the development of breasts, pubic and underarm hair, growth of the genitals, and initiation of menstruation and ovulation.

The Menstrual Cycle and Its Hormones

The inside of the uterus is lined with a layer of tissue called the endometrium. This layer changes form and function when stimulated by two hormones released by certain cells in the ovary.

The menstrual cycle lasts about twenty-eight days, but remember that few women have their period every twenty-eight days. The menstrual cycle varies from woman to woman and factors such as traveling and stress can change the length of the cycle, making it longer or shorter. This is one reason why the rhythm method of birth control is unreliable.

It is helpful to think of the menstrual cycle as divided into two halves. The first half is from the first day of your period to the time of ovulation; the second half is from ovulation to the first day of your next period. Early in the first half, the ovary receives a hormone signal from the pituitary gland (called follicle-stimulating hormone) and a group of follicles inside one or the other of the ovaries begins to grow.

A follicle is a group of cells, one of which is a sex cell. The cells other than the sex cell produce estrogen, which causes the lining of the uterus to grow and become thicker, preparing itself for the implantation of a fertilized egg. When the output of estrogen reaches a certain level, the pituitary reacts by releasing another hormone (called luteinizing hormone) which is the main trigger for ovulation.

Meanwhile, back in the follicle, the sex cell is growing

bigger and becoming an egg—not dividing, but just growing into a very big cell as cells go. At ovulation the egg pops out of the ovary, gets grabbed by the fringe-like end of the uterine tube, and begins its journey down that tube. At about the middle of the tube it stops for a few hours of its twenty-four hour life. If a sperm gets to it in that area in time, fertilization happens. Now we're pregnant. But it all began with hormones.

If there is no follicle-stimulating hormone (FSH), we're not going to get pregnant because the sex cell in the follicle won't grow. This is essentially how "the pill" works. Along with its other functions, estrogen acts as a sort of sedative on the pituitary gland production of FSH. It's a big circle: FSH causes the production of estrogen by way of the follicle; the estrogen gets back to the pituitary to reduce the pituitary's output of FSH in what's called a negative feedback loop. If you make enough estrogen to tell the pituitary not to produce FSH, there's no stimulation of the follicle, no growth of that sex cell, no pregnancy. Given the right amount of estrogen it never fails.

Assuming we did not get pregnant, the unfertilized egg passes down the uterine tube into the uterus and out of the body through the vagina in a trip that takes about a week. In the meantime, following ovulation, those cells in the follicle which had been producing estrogen now start producing another hormone called progesterone. Progesterone finishes the development of the lining of the uterus so that if an egg did get fertilized, the uterus would be ready to receive it and give it a home. Now we're into the second half of the cycle. If we're not pregnant, progesterone will be produced for about twelve days, will suddenly get cut off, and about two days later we will lose the lining of the uterus with accompanying bleeding. This is what we call our period.

If we are pregnant, it is vital that the lining of the uterus not be lost. But when the supply of progesterone drops, the lining of the uterus goes. So how is the progesterone kept flowing? That fertilized egg, that thing that started as a single passive cell in the follicle until the FSH got to it, has now turned into a mass of cells with a will of its own. Now it sends out another hormone (called human chorionic gonadotropin, HCG for short) which keeps the rest of the follicle producing progesterone. (This HCG is found in the blood and the urine and is the basis of many tests of pregnancy. So that's why you're asked for a urine sample when you want a pregnancy test done.) If HCG is present in your urine, then the test will be positive. Progesterone is the hormone of pregnancy. Later, when the placenta develops, progesterone will come from it.

Menstruation usually stops in women between the ages of forty-five and fifty years and this is called menopause. Ovulation also stops. This is normal and due to the fact that the ovaries gradually stop producing hormones even though the pituitary gland is releasing its triggering hormone. Ovulation is often delayed, leading to late periods. In some cycles, ovulation may not occur at all, and in these cycles menstrual bleeding may be heavier than usual. This is a great plan of nature since childbearing late in life would endanger the life of a woman.

Hormones and the Cervix

The cervix, or opening of the uterus, is filled with a thick liquid called mucus which comes from the glands in the cervix. The type and amount of mucus changes at the time of ovulation. The glands of the cervix secrete this mucus constantly but it increases ten times at the time of ovulation, probably due to the increase in estrogen.

During the menstrual cycle, when ovulation is not happening, the mucus is too dense to permit sperm to pass easily through the cervix. At the time of ovulation the mucus becomes less dense (almost exactly like a raw egg white) and sperm can pass through it more easily. This fact is important in fertilization. If sperm are not able to pass through the opening of the uterus, they can hardly combine with an egg. Maybe someday research will find a way of preventing this mucus from changing at the time an ovum can be fertilized, into a clear, thin type: sperm could thus be blocked at the level of the cervix.

How Do These Hormones Work in Men?

Men, like women, produce hormones from the pituitary gland. In fact the hormones that are needed to make an egg pop out of the ovary also are needed to manufacture sperm. And just as these hormones from the pituitary cause estrogen and progesterone to be made by way of the ovary, so do they cause the male hormone testosterone to be made by way of the testicles. Although the contrasts between males and females are nice, we are amazingly similar.

The amount of testosterone a man makes varies on a day-to-day basis but does not rise and fall as sharply as does female hormone production. Both sperm and hormones continue to be made in the testicles throughout a man's lifetime although at lower levels as he grows older.

The major difference between the release of hormones from the pituitary gland into the bloodstream in men and women is that in men they are released continuously. In other words, the pituitary produces a more or less steady flow of hormones which in turn provides a constant signal to the testicles accounting for the continuous production of sperm in the male. On the other hand, the hormones from the pituitary gland affecting ovulation and menstruation in the woman vary.

At puberty males will experience a number of body changes

due to the increased production of hormones. There is a difference in the time the male begins sexual development and the time his genitals will be fully mature. At puberty or at some time during the majority of men's lives their breasts will enlarge. This enlargement can be slight or obvious and often it goes unnoticed. It normally occurs in about fifty percent of males at puberty but does not last for very long and no treatment is necessary. The increase in male and female hormone production in the testicles at this time is possibly responsible for this enlargement.

Breast enlargement in an adult male is not normal, however, and if it is not due to overweight, a physician should be consulted. Although it's uncommon, a man can also develop cancer of the breast.

DEFINITIONS

Female

Mons Pubis. This is the Latin term for the mound of fatty tissue that covers your pubic bone. After puberty, it is covered by crisp, curly hair—the pubic hair.

Vulva. The external female sexual parts are referred to as the vulva, another Latin word. The vulva includes the outer lips (labia majora), the inner lips (labia minora), and the clitoris. The opening to the vagina and the opening to the urethra can be seen when the inner lips are separated.

Labia Majora. This is the Latin term for the major or outer lips of the external genitals of the female. They are folds of skin containing a large amount of fatty tissue. The outer surfaces are covered with pubic hair and the inner surfaces are smooth and hairless. They extend from the mons pubis and border the labia minora. Due to their abundant nerve endings, they are sensitive to the touch.

Labia Minora. This is a Latin term for the minor or inner lips of the female genitals. These are not noticeable before puberty. As the female matures, these folds of skin will develop. They are bright pink and later become brownish in color, and there is little or no hair covering them. The labia minora cover the opening through which urine flows in addition to covering the opening of the vagina. Glands on the inside surface of these folds are called the vestibular glands and they secrete lubricating fluid, particularly when a woman is sexually aroused.

Clitoris (klit̃-or-iss). The clitoris corresponds to the erectile tissue of the penis. It is composed of two small erectile portions and ends with the glans clitoridis. The clitoris is two to three centimeters (more or less one inch) long and generously supplied with sensitive nerve endings. The tip or glans is partially hooded by the junction of the labia minora.

Urethra. Directly below the clitoris is the opening to the urethra. The opening protrudes as an upside-down V-shaped tissue. The urethra is a channel or duct which connects the bladder to the outside. The urethra is not connected to the vagina! It is a completely separate channel which conducts urine from the bladder to the outside of the body.

Hymen. This is a circular or crescent-shaped membrane at the entrance to the vagina. There are great variations in the size, shape, and thickness of this membrane and some women are born without one. In addition, childhood accidents or nor-

mal activity can cause the hymen to tear before the first intercourse.

Vagina. The vagina is a muscular-walled channel capable of
tremendous expansion. It envelops the penis during intercourse, as well as serving as a canal from the uterus to the outside during childbirth. It is three or four inches in length and
expands slightly with sexual stimulation. The vagina is kept
moist with fluid that comes from blood vessels in its wall and
from the glands of the cervix. At puberty, there begins a
growth of bacteria which will live in the vagina until menopause begins. These bacteria are a normal and healthy part of
the environment of the vagina. However, part of the bacterial
population sometimes grows more rapidly and produces an
infection and/or irritation.

Cervix. The cervix is the most narrow portion of the uterus
which projects into the vagina. The cavity of the uterus opens
through the cervix into the vagina. Sperm need to pass through
the cervix in order for fertilization to occur. The cervix can be
felt by putting your finger deeply into your vagina; the cervix
is about the same firmness as the end of your nose.

Uterus. The uterus is a thick-walled, pear-shaped, muscular
organ with a narrow cavity through which sperm pass. It is
the part of the reproductive system that receives the fertilized
egg or ovum from the uterine tubes. The uterus gives the fertilized ovum a place for attachment and then provides all the
blood vessels necessary to nourish the fetus within the
mother's body. In a nonpregnant woman the uterus is about
the size of a small fist, and when pregnancy occurs this organ
is capable of tremendous expansion. About every month the

lining or endometrium of this organ is shed with accompanying bleeding when there is no implantation of a fertilized egg, and this blood makes up the menstrual flow. Womb is another name for the uterus.

Uterine Tubes. There are two uterine tubes. They extend from either side of the rounded upper end of the uterus as trumpet-shaped muscular channels toward the ovaries. These tubes are the part of the female reproductive system that receive the ovum from the ovaries, transport the ovum to the site of fertilization, and then transport the fertilized egg to the uterus. These muscular canals are several inches in length and are open at one end. The open end has fringe-like edges which capture the egg or ovum as it breaks through the surface of the ovary.

Ovaries. There are two ovaries; they are located at the open ends of the uterine tubes. Each is about the size of a small plum and when a woman is born the two together hold some 400,000 follicles. Each follicle contains a female sex cell or ovum. When a follicle matures, it ruptures at the surface of the ovary and releases an ovum.

Male

Scrotum. The scrotum is a sac of skin located behind and below the penis and it contains the testicles. The scrotal skin is loose and thin; it has a wrinkled appearance and a sparse distribution of pubic hair. A lower than normal body temperature is needed for sperm production to occur and that's why the testicles are normally outside the main body cavity. The scrotum serves as a covering for them.

Testicle. The testicles (there are two) are located outside the pelvis and suspended in the scrotum by the spermatic cords. A spermatic cord is composed of a vas deferens, blood vessels, and nerves. The muscles surrounding the spermatic cords raise the testicles in response to fear, cold, and other stimuli. The testicles vary in size but in the adult male they are about the size of a small plum. Each testicle has several hundred tiny compartments filled with tubules which manufacture sperm. The sperm are carried by a series of other tubules to the epididymis. In between the tubules of each testicle are the cells which produce and secrete hormones.

Epididymis. Each epididymis is located within the scrotum and is a tightly coiled tube which curves over the back and top of each testicle. It is the site of storage of sperm. The sperm move slowly through this area and go through a maturing process on their way to the vas deferens.

Vas Deferens. There are two vasa deferentia, one from each testicle. Each is a duct which serves to conduct sperm and connects the epididymis to the urethra. Each vas deferens extends upward into the groin and enters the body cavity where it enters the back of the prostate gland situated below the bladder. Just before entering the prostate, each vas deferens widens and this expanded area is called the ampulla. Although sperm collect in this ampullar area, it must be remembered that sperm are primarily stored in the epididymis as well as some along the entire length of the vasa deferentia.

Seminal Vesicle. Each seminal vesicle (there are two) is an outpocketing of the vas deferens; these pouch-like structures are located behind the bladder and directly below the ampullar portions of the two vas deferens. The contents of the ampulla and the seminal vesicles are emptied into the urethra via a common tube called the ejaculatory duct. The straight ejaculatory ducts pierce the back of the prostate. The purpose of the seminal vesicles is to produce a portion of the seminal fluid which is released into the ejaculatory ducts upon ejaculation.

Prostate Gland. The prostate gland is a firm body about the size of a horse chestnut. It lies directly beneath the bladder surrounding the urethra at the bladder's base. This gland is in a state of continuous activity. Fluid from the prostate is flushed away daily by urine. The prostate gland secretes a portion of the seminal fluid. Ejaculation is a series of events and the prostate is the first to contribute.

Urinary Bladder. The urinary bladder in the male lies behind yet at the same level as the pubic bone. The bladder is a muscular-walled container which expands when filled with urine from the kidney. There is a circular muscle at the base of the bladder. This muscle opens during urination but closes when a man ejaculates. If it did not close during ejaculation, the seminal fluid and sperm would enter the bladder due to the close relationship of the ejaculatory ducts to the opening of the bladder.

Bulbo-Urethral Glands (Cowper's Glands). These glands are located below the prostate gland as outpocketings of the urethra. Each gland is pea-sized and has a duct which empties into the urethra. When a man is sexually aroused, these glands secrete a small amount of clear fluid. This fluid passes down the urethra and out the tip of the penis. Because this small amount of fluid may contain live sperm, unprotected intercourse can result in pregnancy *even if the man does not ejaculate inside the vagina.*

Penis. The human penis contains no bone. The penis is an erectile organ, like the clitoris in the female, and both have the same location. It is composed chiefly of two cylinders of sponge-like tissue which, when filled with blood, cause the penis to become firm and erect. A third cylinder of sponge-like tissue that fits underneath the other two contains the urethra. When the penis is collapsed, there is very little blood in the spaces of these sponge-like tissues. The acorn-shaped tip of the penis is called the glans penis and the urethra opens on the tip of it. In an uncircumcised male, the glans penis is covered by a fold of skin called the foreskin. The foreskin contains glands which produce a white thick fluid called smegma. In uncircumcised males the foreskin should be retracted daily and the smegma washed away with soap and water.

2

CONTRACEPTION

Information about contraceptive methods is becoming more available, access to contraceptives is easier, and women and men are becoming more sophisticated in using them. The pill and other contraceptive methods have brought freedom, but it is biological freedom. Learning about a particular method of contraception and how to use it properly is not as difficult as learning how to understand the effect this biological freedom has on our emotions and our relationships with other people.

Women, as individuals, have wanted freedom from unwanted pregnancy for a long, long time. But the basic facts of how reproduction works were not known until this century; medical technology regarding reproduction has been available only for a few decades. This knowledge and technology have just recently begun to coincide with people's needs and demands. Now we have this freedom, but we have not had it long enough to understand it very well.

Biological freedom means having the number of children you want to have. It means limiting family size, not as a rejection of children, but as an expression of love for them. It

32

means improving the quality of our lives and it leads us to explore the possibilities of other kinds of freedom.

Biological freedom also means having to deal with new roles and new social equations; it involves areas of interaction with other people that have not yet been defined, and involves traditional institutions like marriage that are being redefined. Many of the restraints on feeling, touching, and wanting other people are diminishing. There are a lot of new things to think about. Different social equations, role changes, areas of interaction that are new have had an impact on both men and women. As people feel more free to move out of their traditional roles, they will automatically be faced with new responsibilities.

One social equation many women have grown up with is that intercourse equals pregnancy equals marriage. Therefore, intercourse equals marriage, an equation that has for centuries been a strong part of the foundation of the family unit. But this equation is being challenged now by a new equation: intercourse equals intercourse. While there is nothing new about this for many men, to many women it is an emotional challenge. Some of the expectations they have traditionally linked to intimacy are no longer valid.

Freedom from unwanted pregnancy has freed women to operate in an area that was previously undefined for them. For as obvious as "intercourse equals intercourse" may seem, women have needs beyond those that this equation can satisfy. Girls have been schooled about sex in different ways than boys, and women have different expectations than men. The freedom that contraceptives have brought will allow these expectations to change, but at the same time it puts on women a burden of responsibility for their actions. Women can now define what sexual freedom is for them instead of trying to live up to a definition that was not established by women and does not satisfy their needs. Liberation is as much not feeling guilty about saying "no" as not feeling guilty about saying "yes."

Today virtually all contraceptive methods are effective—in theory. But their success in practice can be quite different. The distinction is between theoretical effectiveness and what is called use-effectiveness. Human beings have made this distinction necessary.

Why do we fail so often? The reasons cover as wide a range as the reasons for failing at any human activity, but some of them are not hard to see: an unacknowledged desire for pregnancy or children; the pressure to fulfill an expected social role as a parent; the illusion that pregnancy can be prevented by an act of will; risk-taking for adventure; wanting to be punished for sex; manipulation of a sex partner; anger towards parents or towards ourselves.

The use-effectiveness of any contraceptive method depends on the action of any number of forces working on us at a particular time in a particular situation. Using any contraceptive method and using it properly requires motivation and initiative. It takes self-discipline, just as it takes discipline and conscious thought not to step off a curb in front of a car.

THE PILL

The birth control pill was first approved by the U.S. Food and Drug Administration in June of 1960. It is now being used by eighty to one hundred million women worldwide, ten to twelve million of them in the United States. Probably no other drug in history has found so many users so fast.

Artificial hormones which give women nearly total control over reproduction have had a staggering impact on women and on our whole society. The immediate acceptance of this particular method of birth control proved the great demand that existed among women for freedom from the burden of unwanted pregnancies.

To obtain this freedom, they needed accurate information on preventing pregnancy and they needed a highly effective method. The technology that created the pill provided the breakthrough. The information on how to get and use it was easily disseminated and the pill works.

Another factor, perhaps more easily overlooked, is the impact of the pill on public policy. For a long time both law and administrative policy have in one way or another acted to suppress information regarding sexual activity and fertility control and to reinforce the social taboos against them. The availability and effectiveness of the pill broke the dam. Once women knew the pill existed there was no way it could be held back. With the availability of the pill and the information on how to use it, suppression of information regarding contraception came to an end.

With the pill women have been given the power to make their own decisions about their reproductive functions, their bodies, their lives. Maybe from the pill came the pressure which has produced reforms in the repressive laws against abortion.

Oral contraceptives, as such, are not new. They have been used for more than 2000 years. The earliest potions contained mercury, arsenic, and strychnine and they probably killed more women than sperm.

In the nineteenth century, a Viennese gynecologist discovered that hormones responsible for female sexual characteristics originated in the ovaries. More than fifty years passed before this knowledge and subsequent research were converted into information useful for the development of oral contraceptives. Dr. Ludwig Haberlandt in 1921 was the first scientist to suggest that hormones from the ovaries might be used as oral contraceptives.

Even then, the application of research to contraceptive development was resisted by drug companies because they were afraid of controversy. A grant to the Worcester Foundation in 1951 by Margaret Sanger and her allies no doubt speeded the development of the first oral contraceptive available to the general public. In addition, the synthesis in 1952 of a female hormone (progestin) which could be taken orally was crucial because natural hormones were expensive.

Synthetic estrogens and progesterones were approved by the U.S. Food and Drug Administration (FDA) in 1957 for the treatment of menstrual disorders but not as oral contraceptives. It was one thing to approve a drug for women with menstrual problems; it was another thing to approve a drug to be used by healthy women over a long period of time.

The first birth control pill, a combination of estrogen and progestin, was approved by the FDA in June of 1960. It was easy to take, reversible, not associated with the sex act, was nearly one hundred percent effective, and had other beneficial effects such as regulation of a woman's menstrual cycle. In the years since 1960, we have witnessed "the pill scare," discussion, controversy, research, evaluation—all positive and negative aspects of this contraceptive revolution.

There are certainly risks associated with the use of the pill. But the risks are outweighed by the benefits for most women. The risks with the pill, as with all contraceptives, must be weighed against the risks to the life and health of the woman becoming pregnant and giving birth.

There has been a lot of information about the possible dangers of oral contraceptives, which has led to a lot of anxiety among women who have used them successfully for years. Unfortunately, the comparison of these dangers to the dangers of pregnancy is not usually made. For when the risks of pregnancy are considered, oral contraceptives are far safer for a woman than a less effective method of contraception or a method that is used less effectively. As far as overall health is concerned, a report called *Oral Contraceptives and Health* issued by the Royal College of General Practitioners in Great Britain says, "The evidence suggests . . . that oral contraceptive users suffer in total no more episodes of illness than nonusers, and they may actually have less."

There are two types of oral contraceptives in use at this time—the combination pill with specific dosages of synthetic estrogen and progesterone, and the "minipill" containing a specific dosage of synthetic progesterone only. (Progesterone is the name of the natural hormone and progestin is the name of the synthetic hormone.)

The synthetic hormones of the combination pill replace a woman's own female hormones, estrogen and progesterone. Estrogen is produced by follicles inside the ovary. After ovulation, the remainder of the follicle produces progesterone plus some estrogen.

In order for a follicle inside one or the other ovary to begin to grow there must be a signal from the pituitary gland transported by the bloodstream to the ovary. When the ovary receives this signal, a group of follicles will begin to grow and produce estrogen. The interaction of estrogen and the hormone signal from the pituitary can be likened to a child's seesaw. As one goes up, the other comes down. As the production of estrogen increases, the hormone signal from the pituitary decreases and no more follicles are stimulated.

This lack of growth of a follicle is exactly what occurs during pregnancy when estrogen and progesterone are made by the placenta to prevent the pituitary gland from releasing the hormone signal that stimulates follicle growth. So a pregnancy-like situation is established by taking the combination-type oral contraceptives. (And pregnancy-like body changes occur, such as enlarged or tender breasts, fullness, nausea, weight gain or loss, and so on.)

Now you're probably thinking that if the birth control pill stops ovulation it should stop menstruation. There is a similarity to pregnancy here, also. When a woman gives birth, the levels of estrogen and progesterone fall sharply and the lining of the uterus separates from the mother. Birth control pills are taken for twenty or twenty-one days, and when a woman stops taking them, the levels of estrogen and progesterone fall. The lining of the uterus is lost; this is the menstrual flow.

The fifth day after the beginning of the menstrual flow, the woman begins taking birth control pills once again. If she doesn't, the pituitary gland will signal the ovary to develop a follicle.

Some women forgot to begin taking their pill again after they menstruated and they sometimes got pregnant. Consequently, some manufacturers included seven additional pills for each twenty-one hormone pills in a month's supply. These additional pills are inactive; in other words they contain no hormones. Sometimes, though, they contain an iron supplement, like a vitamin pill. When twenty-eight pills are included in a package, a woman takes one pill every single day. First she is taking the twenty-one "active" pills and then the seven "inactive" pills. During several of the seven days the inactive pills are being taken, menstruation occurs. Obviously, with the twenty-eight pill packages, it is vital that the pills be taken in the right order and that a woman doesn't skip around.

There is little disagreement that oral contraceptives, used properly, have the lowest failure rate of any reversible method of contraception. The combination pill is nearly a hundred percent effective. This, of course, is only true when a woman takes a birth control pill *every* day (for the prescribed twenty-one or twenty-eight days) and preferably at the same time during the day. The hormones in each pill last twenty-four hours in the body. Then another pill must be taken. Taking a pill at the same time each day is particularly important for low-dosage pills. Try to associate swallowing a pill with dinner or other regular activity.

If pills are skipped, the hormone levels in the body will fall. In two to four days, bleeding or spotting will usually occur for the same reason that menstruation occurs when a woman finishes taking a whole month's packet of pills. If you miss one pill take it as soon as you remember; if two pills are missed take two pills as soon as you remember and then two the next day to get yourself back on schedule. But if two are missed, use another contraceptive method until that packet of pills is finished. In any case, if pills are skipped and you do not menstruate call a doctor or clinic and ask about a pregnancy test. If you are following instructions and still experiencing spotting or bleeding between periods or are missing one or more periods call your physician or clinic and explain the problem.

Because directions are not always followed, various studies found from one to seven pregnancies occurring for every hundred women taking combination oral contraceptives for one year. (New users should use a second method of birth control, for example foam and condom, during the first month they are on the pill.)

Remember that when you see a doctor for other problems, be sure to mention that you are taking birth control pills.

The pill has positive as well as negative side effects. Most women find their menstrual cycle more predictable. After taking twenty or twenty-one hormonal pills, menstruation will follow in two to four days. The flow is usually shorter and lighter than before, particularly with the lower dosage pills. This is because the lining of the uterus does not develop fully and the result is less blood loss. For an undernourished or anemic woman, this decreased blood flow is a distinct advantage. In addition, for most women, there is less cramping and premenstrual tension.

One out of every eighteen women in the United States dies of breast cancer. Both cancerous and noncancerous breast disease are related to hormonal conditions. Because of this relationship, R. Hertz, in 1969, recommended that the possible effects of oral contraceptives on breast disease be carefully studied. As pointed out in *Population Reports* published by the Population Information Program of George Washington University Medical Center, studies to date which have been done are "reassuring and suggest beneficial or protective effects are as likely—or indeed more likely—than adverse effects." Although the studies which have been done do not prove that taking oral contraceptives will prevent later breast disease, they are encouraging.

Usually the side effects noticed first by a woman taking the pill are nausea, vomiting, dizziness, headaches, enlarged or tender breasts, fluid retention, weight gain, or breakthrough bleeding. A woman might experience all of these, just one or two, or none. These side effects are usually reduced with the lower dosage combination pill. A new pill user can take her pill at bedtime or with dinner to reduce the effect of nausea. As the body becomes conditioned to this new hormone regulation, such symptoms disappear—usually within two to three months. Other effects may be depression; change in libido; increased appetite; fatigue; and more problems with yeast infection, vaginal itching, or discharge.

There has been concern about the possible association of cancer of the cervix or uterus and pill-taking. The latest studies show no connection between cancer of the cervix and use of the pill.

As for uterine cancer, the Obstetrics and Gynecology Committee of the FDA has recently stated that "there appears to be a higher risk of endometrial cancer (cancer of the lining of the uterus) in association with the long-term use of estrogens in post menopausal women." With this evidence of the association between uterine cancer and the long-term use of estrogens for reasons other than birth control in women past menopause, the possibility of such an association in women who have been using estrogen for birth control for a long period of time must be at least considered. The FDA has proposed that a brochure containing this information be given to women taking oral contraceptives containing estrogen.

There is no doubt of the connection between use of the pill and certain blood clotting disorders. While these disorders are uncommon, it is important to know what they are and their warning signs.

Thrombophlebitis (inflammation of a vein wall) usually causes pain, tenderness, warmth, redness, and sometimes swelling—symptoms usually noticed in the leg.

Pulmonary embolism (deposit of a blood clot, usually from the leg, in an artery of the lung) causes more or less severe chest pain, difficulty in breathing, and anxiety.

Cerebral thrombosis (stroke, the closing-off of a blood vessel in the head) can cause weakness, paralysis, or loss of sensation on one side of the body; difficulty in speech; and may be accompanied by dizziness, headache, and vomiting.

Coronary thrombosis (heart attack) is accompanied by severe squeezing or pressing pain in the chest, difficulty in breathing, weakness, and sweating.

Although anyone taking the pill should be aware of these warning signs, they should understand that these serious medical problems are relatively uncommon. As far as is known, for most women, the benefits of the pill outweigh the risks. The statistics are hard to understand without understanding and comparing the seriousness of each medical problem, the different amounts of estrogen in different pills, or the age and other factors related to the person taking the pill. It is possible that the risks have received a disproportionate amount of attention in the media compared to the benefits.

On the other hand, it is important for women over forty who take the pill to know that evidence indicates they have a significantly greater risk of heart attack, particularly if they smoke, are overweight or diabetic, have hypertension or high cholesterol levels. The FDA Obstetrics and Gynecology Advisory Committee has recommended that women over forty be made aware of this increased risk. Other researchers have stressed that women in this situation should discuss it with their doctors.

Women using the pill should be sure to have their blood pressure checked every few months during the first year of use and regularly after that. Higher blood pressure is one possible side effect. If the pressure is above 140/90 (ask the person taking it to explain), the pill is usually discontinued. The blood pressure usually returns to normal once the woman stops taking the pill.

As an example of how thoroughly oral contraceptives have been researched, the report, *Oral Contraceptives and Health,* by the Royal College of General Practitioners showed that a woman taking combined oral contraceptives would not need to have her ears syringed for wax as often as if she didn't take the pill, although she is not likely to be impressed if she is faced with hypertension due to the drug.

Several studies suggest, *but do not prove,* that oral contraceptives may also be associated with diabetes, liver tumors, gall bladder disease, urinary tract infections and vaginal discharge, and skin changes.

Women should not take oral contraceptives or other drugs during pregnancy. If a woman has not taken the pill as directed and has missed a period, she should eliminate the possibility that she is pregnant before she takes a second month's supply of pills. This is to avoid the risk of damage that might be done to the developing fetus by the drug.

Women who wish to become pregnant should consider waiting for about three months after stopping the pill before getting pregnant. There is the possibility of increased risk of spontaneous abortion in women who become pregnant shortly after discontinuing the pill.

The second kind of birth control pill is the "minipill," which contains only the synthetic hormone progestin, the name for the synthetic form of the naturally occurring form of the hormone, progesterone. The exact way in which it works is not as well understood as the combination pill. The way it works depends on the amount of hormone, the kind of progestin, and the woman's own body chemistry. Unlike combined orals, a hormonally active minipill is taken every day without stopping, even during menstruation.

In general terms, the minipill prevents ovulation some of the time, decreases the speed at which the egg moves through the uterine tube, changes the quality of the cervical mucus so as to make it more difficult for the sperm to move into the uterus, and changes the lining of the uterus so a fertilized egg cannot implant itself.

The minipill only prevents ovulation in some women (up to forty percent) during some menstrual cycles because the hormone signal from the pituitary gland that triggers the growth of a follicle is not shut off. (Estrogen is the hormone which shuts down this chemical trigger and the minipill doesn't contain any estrogen.) The hormone signal that induces ovulation is not shut off either, but is altered by the progestin in the minipill and consequently ovulation sometimes happens. The follicles in the ovary are stimulated to develop by the follicle-stimulating hormone (FSH) from the pituitary gland but they may never release an egg.

Even if an ovum is released there are other effects of this pill that prevent implantation by making the lining of the uterus unsuitable, by slowing the movement of sperm through the cervix by making the cervical mucus too thick, by altering the speed of the ovum through the uterine tubes, and by causing disruption of the progesterone secretion in the ovary. So in the minipill there are several mechanisms at work, unlike the single mechanism of the combination pill. The effectiveness of the minipill is less than that of combined oral contraceptives, but about the same as the IUD. Because pregnancy rates are highest in the first six months, new minipill users are urged to use a second method during this time.

When taking minipills it is very important to take a pill every day. A pregnancy can result from missing only one or two pills. Missing a pill includes losing a pill while vomiting.

An ectopic pregnancy is any fertilized egg developing outside the uterus, in a uterine tube for example. Since the combination oral contraceptives prevent ovulation, ectopic pregnancies do not occur. The minipill many times does not prevent ovulation; it prevents implantation of a fertilized egg in most cases. But when it fails and implantation does occur, it is more likely to occur outside the uterus, that is, as an ectopic pregnancy, than if a woman was not using any contraceptive method. This is because the minipill slows the speed of the egg moving through the uterine tube and makes implantation there more likely. It therefore is less effective in preventing tubal pregnancies than uterine pregnancies. (This is also true of the IUD.)

If a woman is taking minipills and has pain in her abdomen, she should seek medical help immediately. The uterine tube is about one-half centimeter in diameter and the developing fertilized egg will put more and more pressure on this small tube.

The minipill was first marketed in January, 1973, to fill the need for an oral contraceptive that did not have the negative side effects of combined oral contraceptives. However, menstrual irregularity has proven to be a significant drawback to its popularity. It can increase or decrease the flow, shorten or lengthen cycles, and result in spotting or bleeding between periods. The minipill is most suitable for women whose bodies are sensitive to combined oral contraceptives and can be prescribed for those who are nursing because it does not interfere with the quantity or length of milk production. However, the high incidence of bleeding between periods has led to so much dissatisfaction among women that it is not generally prescribed.

The sequential birth control pills Oracon, Ortho-Novum SQ, and Norquen have been removed from the market by the FDA. It is estimated that at the time of their removal in February, 1976, 5 to 10 percent of the ten million women taking oral contraceptives were taking them. Sequential birth control pills contain estrogen alone for most of the pill-taking cycle, and an estrogen and progestin for the remaining part of the cycle, whereas the combination pills combine estrogen and progestin for the entire three-week cycle.

The FDA decided that sequentials should be removed from the market after concluding:

"They are somewhat less effective than combination birth

control pills; they are associated with a higher risk of blood clotting than the combination pills; and they appear to have the potential for higher risk of cancer of the uterus than the combination pills. Women who are taking sequentials should finish out their cycles and contact their physicians for a prescription for a different birth control pill, or select another method of contraception."

Injectable Contraceptives—"The Shot"

"The Shot" is a type of hormone (progestin) which works like the minipill in preventing pregnancy.

There is a good deal of controversy over injectable contraceptives. The two major concerns are the possibility of infertility after use and a possible link with cancer of the cervix. Although "the shot" is currently marketed in sixty-four countries, the injectable Depo-Provera (Upjohn Co.) has not yet gained the approval of the U.S. Food and Drug Administration for general use in the United States. The approval of the drug is still in the investigational stage, studies are continuing, and more data is needed before approval will be granted. At this time, it is obtainable in the U.S. with a woman's signed consent.

Some women prefer this method of contraception because they don't want to take a pill daily but do want something as effective as combined oral contraceptives. Others have experienced estrogen-related side effects or have become pregnant using other methods. It has also been used as a contraceptive for the retarded.

If a woman or couple choose this method, they are advised to use a back-up contraceptive for the first two weeks after the first shot. After the first shot, she should make an appointment in three months for the next injection and, as with oral contraceptives, report any dizziness, loss of sight, strong leg or chest pain, or difficulty in breathing to her doctor immediately.

Injectables offer about the same high degree of effectiveness as combined oral contraceptives. They are injected two or four times per year so they are appealing for their long-lasting effects. They do not reduce the supply of milk in nursing mothers, although whether the milk is changed or whether the drug affects the infant is not certain. On the other hand, injectables disrupt menstrual patterns as does the minipill. By the end of two years, 40 percent or more of Depo-Provera users are amenorrheic, that is, they are not menstruating. The shot is not advised for women already experiencing undiagnosed abnormal bleeding or women who are at the end of their reproductive years—a time when irregular menstrual bleeding produced by the shot could not be distinguished from bleeding which may be an early warning sign of uterine or cervical cancer.

Acceptance of this contraceptive has been hindered by the still unanswered questions of permanent infertility and cancer, and any woman wishing to use this method of birth control ought to inform herself. Because of the development of breast tumors in experimental animals when given injectable progestins, women are also urged to be sure to do monthly breast exams when they use this drug.

THE IUD

Today the intrauterine device, the IUD, is one of the major methods of birth control. It, like the pill, was a scientific advance that brought tremendous social change. It is estimated that about fifteen million women in the world use the device, three to four million of them in the United States.

The IUD has appeal because it is essentially a one-shot

operation. Except for checking its strings each month after your period, you have nothing to do. If a woman doesn't want to keep thinking about contraception, even to the extent of taking a pill every day, if she just wants to "set it and forget it," the IUD is ideal.

Unfortunately, some women's bodies will tolerate the device and some will not. Women who have not had children are more likely to have problems with it. A uterus which has not been stretched by pregnancy is more likely to expel the device. Some women have experienced such problems as abdominal pain and infection. Most women experience increased bleeding during their periods. Other women object to the IUD simply because it is a foreign object introduced into the body and nobody knows for sure how or why it works or what its long-term effects may be. But despite the objections and drawbacks, the IUD is a highly effective alternative for some women and a necessary option for others who cannot use other methods for whatever reason.

Even for women who have no problems with the IUD, though, the device is less effective than sterilization or the birth control pill. There have been as many as six pregnancies among every hundred women using it for one year. Women who must not become pregnant should not depend upon the IUD unless abortion is an acceptable option.

Pregnancy can occur while the IUD is in place or after the IUD has been expelled without the woman's knowledge. Expulsion will most often take place during menstruation when the opening to the cervix is slightly larger than usual and the cramps that often go with menstruation can mask the cramps that would accompany the loss of the IUD. (In general, larger IUDs are less likely to be lost, though smaller ones do cause less bleeding and pain.)

Much has been learned about IUDs since their first widespread acceptance in the 1960s, and about two dozen different types have now been invented. As stated in *Population Reports*, IUDs Reassessed, A Decade of Experience, "the apparent difference in performance between one device and another is often not as great as the difference between one clinical center and another. In other words, the skill of the person performing the insertion, the quality of counseling, reassurance, and follow-up, and the cultural setting of the program may be more important than minor changes in the device."

The name for the device came from the fact that it stays within (intra) the uterus. The idea of putting a foreign object in the uterus to prevent pregnancy has been around for a long time. It is said that camel drivers put small pebbles or date pits into the camel uterus to prevent pregnancy during long journeys. It is not said how many camels died of infection as a result.

Pelvic infection, in fact, kept the IUD in disrepute for women, or at least limited its acceptance, until the creation of antibiotics. Essentially it was developed by trial and error. Contraception was not orginally the main purpose; the intention was to regulate menstruation, relieve menstrual pain, support the uterus, or cure infertility. In the majority of cases it also prevented pregnancy. Many early IUDs were made of valuable materials such as ivory, silver, gold, and diamond-studded platinum. Great for a wedding gift.

The first device designed specifically for contraception was made of silkworm gut, in 1909, by a German physician named Richter. Later designs made of metal were condemned by physicians, and widespread acceptance was delayed until Jack Lippes introduced his plastic Lippes Loop at an international conference in 1962. Since that time, use of the IUD has increased enormously.

Today's device, made of plastic, plastic plus metal, or plastic plus hormone, is put into the uterus by a physician or women's health care specialist to prevent pregnancy; it is removed when a woman wants to get pregnant. It may be a loop, coil, or any of a variety of shapes, and each new one is advertised to work better than the others.

The devices most commonly used at this time are named Lippes Loop, Saf-T-Coil, Copper-T, and Copper-7. The Dalkon Shield has been removed from the market but the U.S. Food and Drug Administration says that physicians don't have to remove a Dalkon Shield if the woman is not pregnant and if she does not have any problems with it. *Be sure to know what kind of IUD you have.*

There is no single opinion on how the IUD prevents pregnancy. The most generally accepted theory is that it prevents implantation of the fertilized egg in the wall of the uterus. This may be caused by a reaction of the cells in the uterus to a foreign object. It has also been found that the uterine fluid in women wearing an IUD changes, causing the uterus to reject the ball of cells formed from the fertilized egg. Several researchers have suggested that the presence of the IUD produces motion of the uterine tubes, which changes the speed at which the fertilized egg travels towards the uterus so it doesn't get there at the right time for implantation. Finally, the IUD somehow interferes with the movement of sperm into the uterine tubes so the chance of fertilization taking place is somewhat reduced.

But the important thing to understand about the IUD is that, unlike the pill, the condom, the diaphragm, and vaginal contraceptives, it does not prevent fertilization: it prevents the implantation of the fertilized egg, the point at which pregnancy may be said to begin.

Women who are considering an IUD as a contraceptive

should begin with a complete pelvic exam to make sure that the cervix, uterus, uterine tubes, and ovaries are normal and healthy. Those who have a history of infections in their ovaries, uterine tubes, or uterus may experience a recurrence of infection following insertion. Those who have had cervical or uterine cancer, who have cervicitis (an inflammation of the cervix), those who have or think they may have a sexually transmitted disease—none of them should have an IUD. Women with an unusually shaped or unusually small uterus cannot use this device.

Unlike the pill, the IUD does not regulate the menstrual cycle, and if a woman was irregular before the insertion of the IUD she can expect the same pattern but with increase in the days and amount of flow. Therefore women who normally have heavy bleeding or are anemic should not have an IUD. Those who experience pain during their menstrual period should not have one either. Like the heavy flow, it just makes things worse.

There are serious risks if the IUD is inserted while a woman is pregnant. To guard against these risks the IUD is inserted at times when the woman is obviously not pregnant—in the last days of menstruation, immediately after childbirth, or after an abortion. At these times, also, the cervix is slightly wider and a bit softer. Not all health care professionals agree about inserting an IUD immediately after childbirth or abortion. There is speculation that inserting a device at this time, when the uterus is enlarged and relatively soft, may result in the device imbedding in the uterine tissue when the uterus returns to normal. Some believe that short-term contraception should be used for at least six to eight weeks before IUD insertion.

For insertion, a simple instrument called a speculum is placed in the vagina to separate the vaginal walls and to make the cervix visible. Because the cervical opening is so small, the

IUD is packaged with a special inserter that straightens its looped, coiled, or otherwise bent shape. The practitioner pushes the inserter and IUD into the cervical canal which leads to the uterus. Once inside the uterine cavity, it is released from the inserter and the inserter removed. The device is now in place.

Generally, no anesthetic is used for the insertion. The diameter of the inserter and the stretched or unstretched state of the cervix usually determine whether or not there is pain. Women who have not had any children may experience considerable pain as the insertion of the IUD stretches the cervical canal. Some physicians routinely numb the cervix before insertion.

For five days after insertion it's unwise to have sexual intercourse. The uterus needs a chance to overcome the trauma of insertion and to regain some resistance to infection. There is evidence to support a two and one-half to nine percent increase in pelvic inflammatory disease (PID—inflammation of the uterus or uterine tubes) with IUD use. This increase does not seem to be dependent on the length of time the IUD is in place nor how many sexual partners a woman has.

Signs of infection, if it should occur, include an oral temperature of 99.8 degrees F. or higher; tenderness in the lower abdomen between menstrual periods and progressively more painful periods; menstrual bleeding progressively longer and intermenstrual bleeding occurring after you have had your IUD in place for longer than three months; painful intercourse, particularly when the penis is pushed deeply into the vagina or when the vagina is pushed onto the penis; and vaginal discharge of increasing amount or with unsual odor.

The most common complication of insertion is perforation of the uterus. The channel of the uterus is very narrow and placing an object in this channel at a precise angle requires skill and experience. While perforation of the uterus during insertion is not common, the risk is real enough to warrant careful consideration of who will insert your IUD. The average general practitioner is not qualified.

Expulsion of the IUD is most likely during the first three months after the device has been inserted. It is important during these first three months to check the strings of the IUD each week, or to check them before relying on the IUD for protection. There is a plastic string that hangs down into the upper vagina so you can check the IUD to be sure it is in place. After three months you should at least check the device after every period or any time you have abdominal cramping.

This is most easily done in a squatting position. Put your finger into your vagina and feel for the cervix. Push deeply into the vagina until a round bump is felt about the same firmness as the tip of your nose. Now try to feel the strings coming out the center of it. Do not pull them. If any part of the IUD other than the strings can be felt, the IUD is not completely inside the uterus. Also, a change in the length of the strings is a warning signal. In these cases, the body is rejecting the device through the cervical canal; see your practitioner or go to a clinic. Do not try to remove the device yourself! If a woman cannot feel the strings, she can ask her partner to check them for her. He will often be able to feel the cervix more easily than she can. When either the body of the IUD is felt or the strings cannot be felt, use another form of contraception *before* having intercourse. For example, foam and a condom can be used. It is advised that you also use a back-up method for the first three months you have an IUD. And, some women routinely use foam during mid-cycle as added protection.

Although a woman's age and the number of children she has will be the major factors in determining whether her body tolerates an IUD, a woman who has had no children seems to experience less rejection with the IUD that consists of copper wound around a plastic base. The copper is believed to increase the effectiveness of the device. Since the copper dissolves over a period of time the device must be replaced every two years.

The prolonged effects of copper dissolving within the body are not known. Women who have a known or suspected sensitivity to copper should not use this device. Microwave therapy of the abdominal or lower back areas should not be used in women wearing a copper IUD; the treatment may cause heat injury to the surrounding uterine tissues. Because the copper may be absorbed into the bloodstream, all IUDs with copper have been made subject to regulation by the U.S. Food and Drug Administration. IUDs without metal or hormones are considered devices rather than drugs and are not under the same kind of regulation.

Although, to date, no relationship between cancer or infection and the copper IUD has been established, more study needs to be done on the effect of copper on the body. Studies of long-term effects of copper on future pregnancies are not yet available. Although IUDs as a whole are considered to be a relatively safe and reliable means of contraception, the FDA report on the Current Status of IUD Investigation noted that "existing data are insufficient to permit a thorough scientific review of the safety and adequacy of IUD contraceptive devices."

The newest type of IUD is made of plastic that contains a hormone which is released gradually into the uterus, supposedly increasing the effectiveness of the device. It must be replaced every year. The developers of this IUD, called Progestasert, do not claim to have solved the problems of the side effects common to all IUDs.

The IUD is a temporary contraceptive and, as far as we know, its effects are completely reversible. Using an IUD drastically reduces your chances of getting pregnant; having it removed restores your chances to what they were before. The procedure for removing it is a medical one and must be done by a skilled practitioner. While it is simply a matter of pulling it out, there is a risk of damage to the cervix and surrounding area if it is not done properly.

The most obvious reason for having the IUD removed is the desire to have a baby. There are other medical reasons why it should be removed. The side effects of the IUD, such as increased menstrual flow, spotting between periods, pain (cramping), or infection, are unacceptable to many women and for one or more of these reasons they will have the device removed. The side effects of increased bleeding, cramping, and spotting are more common in the first three months after insertion. The increased blood loss is a significant problem for women who are anemic or have poor diets. Yearly exams for women wearing an IUD should include a hematocrit test which checks to see if their blood contains a a normal amount of red blood cells.

The IUD is not one hundred percent effective. A woman can still become pregnant even though she has an IUD in place. If she does become pregnant, it is absolutely necessary that she consult a physician right away about having the IUD removed, whether she wants to have the child or not. If the device is not removed, she runs a risk of serious infection which can be fatal. An FDA bulletin states: "Patients with an IUD in place who miss their normal menstrual period or who become pregnant should seek medical advice at the earliest possible time."

Since the IUD in most cases prevents implantation of a fertilized egg rather than fertilization, there is a greater than usual risk that if pregnancy does occur, it will take place out-

side the uterus. The medical term for this is an ectopic pregnancy. The fertilized egg implants itself in the uterine tube or
on an ovary and begins to develop. The pain from the pressure
of the growing embryo will be one of the first signs that something is wrong, as will a missed period. This is another reason
why a woman wearing an IUD should seek medical help
immediately if pain or a missed period occurs.

DIAPHRAGM AND JELLY OR CREAM

In the early 1960s, before the majority of women turned
to the birth control pill and the IUD, the diaphragm was used
by more than half the women in the United States. Its popularity dropped as the ease, convenience, and effectiveness of
the pill and the IUD became well known.

But negative publicity about oral contraceptives and the
IUD has turned women to the diaphragm once more. They
have now gained greater knowledge of their bodies' reproductive structures and are less reluctant about touching their
genitals, due, in part, to the widespread use of tampons.
Many women find the diaphragm a convenient short-term
method of birth control. In addition, it is excellent for women
who are nursing. They can be assured no hormones are inter-
fering with milk production.

It has been said that the diaphragm should be used by those
women or couples who are sure they don't want to have any
children, for its effectiveness is greatly dependent on personal
motivation. If you tend to screw up a lot, forget, or feel
ambivalent about contraception, this is not the method for
you.

One reason why women who are dissatisfied with other
methods have turned to the diaphragm is that it is a positive
statement about intercourse. In contrast to taking pills, a fairly
passive action that becomes, to many, a habit, like brushing

your teeth, using the diaphragm calls for an active decision. It is linked with the person you are going to bed with, how you feel about him at that moment, how you feel about intercourse with him, and how you feel about protecting yourself from pregnancy. As for the argument that this method interrupts the sex act, women have found that, in anticipation of intercourse, they can insert the diaphragm ahead of time, in the middle of the evening, to lessen anxiety about excusing themselves in the middle of foreplay. Other women, having used the diaphragm for years, are perfectly comfortable inserting it in front of their partner or having their partner do the inserting.

The diaphragm is a cup-shaped device you insert into the vagina before intercourse. It covers the cervix and prevents sperm from entering the uterus. The idea has been around a long time.

Casanova recommended squeezing half a lemon and inserting it into the vagina to cover the cervix. The lemon shell acted as a barrier to sperm and the lemon juice as a spermicide. Other materials, such as oiled, silky paper used by the Chinese and Japanese; opium molded into a cup shape by women of Sumatra; gums, leaves, sponges, and who knows what else, were also inserted into the vagina in hope of stopping sperm from entering the cervix.

A German physician invented the modern-day diaphragm and described it in an article, in 1882, which he signed with a phony name to protect his reputation. The use of this method spread to Holland and then to England. It not only was an effective contraceptive. but for the first time gave women reliable control of contraception.

The modern diaphragm is shaped like a cup or dome of thin, soft rubber with a circular plastic or metal rim. This rim can be pressed into a narrow oval shape for easy insertion into the vagina just as a tampon would be inserted. Once in place behind the pubic bone, it springs back into its circular shape and cannot be felt. In addition, the diaphragm is rarely felt by the woman's partner during intercourse.

Since every woman's body is different and since a practitioner's authorization is needed to buy a diaphragm, a women's health care specialist or physician must be consulted. Fitting takes time and most physicians are very busy; a women's health care specialist is likely to have more time to spend with a woman to encourage her and to make certain, *before she leaves the office or clinic,* that she understands how to insert and remove the diaphragm.

The diaphragm must fit the upper part of the vagina snugly; if it is not fitted properly, or if the size of the upper vagina, where the diaphragm rests, should change, the cervix could be exposed to sperm during intercourse.

Change can occur after a woman gains or loses fifteen or more pounds, after miscarriage or childbirth, after an abortion, after the first intercourse, or after an operation.

If the diaphragm is too tight it can slip out from under the pubic bone; if it is too loose, it can be pushed out of place by the penis. In addition, a diaphragm that is too tight can cause pressure on the urethra which then causes pain or difficulty upon urination. If a woman experiences pain or difficult urination while wearing the diaphragm, she should see a women's health care specialist or a physician who is knowledgeable in fitting diaphragms.

Physicians are health care consumers, too, and they have their own biases towards contraceptives. These biases can stem from personal or from professional experience. The practitioner may not be comfortable prescribing this method because of ignorance. Unfortunately, many health professionals assume women would rather take a pill every day or have an IUD and check strings once a month than use a diaphragm every time they have intercourse. If a woman or couple want to use this method and are confronted with a physician who is evasive or puts it down, they shouldn't be discouraged. Many doctors complete their training with little or no experience in fitting diaphragms.

To be effective, the diaphragm must be used with a spermicidal jelly or cream which is placed inside the dome and around the rim of the dome. Both can be purchased without a prescription at almost any drug store. Either one is fine; jelly gives more lubrication. There are a few brands of spermicide that are potentially harmful because they contain organic mercury. Check the label and avoid these.

The diaphragm and spermicide act in two ways. The diaphragm is a mechanical barrier and the spermicide is a backup, chemical barrier. Sperm can easily slip around the rim of the diaphragm no matter how snugly it fits. Therefore, the spermicide is *absolutely* necessary with the diaphragm, for protection. Do not substitute petroleum jelly (Vaseline) or other lubricants. They don't work because they do not kill sperm.

Don't rely on the diaphragm without the spermicide. If you've emptied your last tube of cream or jelly and the drugstores are closed, postpone intercourse! Or have your partner use a condom. There is no such thing as being half pregnant.

When a properly fitted diaphragm without defects is inserted correctly and used with cream or jelly *every* time a woman has intercourse, it is 97% effective. However, there are more pregnancies than that with this method because of incorrect insertion, failure to use jelly or cream, or failure to leave the diaphragm in place at least six hours after intercourse.

If you are using a diaphragm for the first time, allow yourself plenty of time to insert it. If you have difficulty inserting it, don't be surprised, because everyone usually does. It takes time to get to know the inside of your vagina, to find the cervix and the "shelf" that the pubic bone makes.

Urinate first. The bladder is just above the pubic bone, which, along with the muscles of the vagina, holds the diaphragm in place. If the bladder is full, placing the diaphragm is more difficult and pressure on the bladder is uncomfortable.

Now apply a large teaspoonful of cream or jelly inside the dome. Spread the jelly on the inside of the dome around the rim and some on the outside if you wish. Remember though, that the inside of the dome will be against the cervix and this is where most of the jelly will be needed. Don't smear too much jelly on the rim; you need an effective seal but a thick layer could cause the rim to slide.

Now take the rim in one hand between the thumb and the forefinger and pinch the diaphragm into a narrow oval shape. Sitting with your legs apart (perhaps on the toilet), standing with one leg up on a chair or bathtub, or squatting, use your free hand to spread the folds of skin which cover the vaginal opening. With the dome bulging downward, insert the diaphram like a tampon. Help it along the vagina by pushing back and up on the rim. (Remember, the vagina is at an angle toward the small of the back.) Once it is far enough into the vagina, use your finger to tuck the rim over the "shelf" the pubic bone makes. Some women find an inserter, which is a plastic device that folds and holds the diaphragm, more convenient. It can be bought with the diaphragm.

Check to see if the diaphragm covers the cervix by reaching into the vagina with your middle finger. The cervix feels like a bump deep in the vagina and has the same firmness as the end of your nose. It will be difficult to reach unless you are sitting or in a squatting position.

To remove the diaphragm, put a forefinger or middle finger

into the vagina, crook it under the rim at the pubic bone, and gently pull the diaphragm down and out.

Some women insert a diaphragm comfortably in front of their partner, or with his help, but not all women do. The kind of relationship you have will determine whether or not you need to figure out how and when to do it. We all have our own ideas on sexual etiquette; being intimate is delicate and we can feel vulnerable at times. We all get behavorial cues from others as we grow up; our parents guide us through table manners and being polite, but neither they nor Amy Vanderbilt have given us any guidelines in regard to contra-cepting ourselves.

If you are spending the day with a man you've just recently met but are very attracted to, should you take along your diaphragm just in case? If passion develops, do you keep your handbag clutched at your side? Do you casually leave the dia-phragm in the bathroom so you can go there later and insert it? There are no perfect answers. One idea is to ask the person you are going to make love with how he would feel if you got pregnant. Perhaps this is not terribly romantic, but neither is an unwanted pregnancy. Of course, many men will auto-matically bring up the subject, which is great, and then you can say you use the diaphragm.

You can insert the diaphragm ahead of the time you need it, but if more than two hours have passed, use an applicator full of foam or jelly before intercourse. After inserting the diaphragm, you can walk around, take a bath, or urinate with it in place. If you have a bowel movement, the diaphragm might become dislodged, though, so you will need to check its position. If you look at a side view of the female sexual organs, you'll notice that the rectum lies directly behind one surface where the diaphragm rests. If the bowel is full when the diaphragm is inserted and the bowel is then emptied, the area around the diaphragm becomes larger, which can shift the diaphragm and expose the cervix to sperm.

Some medical people recommend an additional application of spermicidal cream or jelly after *each* intercourse while the diaphragm is in place. Others feel this additional application is unnecessary. The original cream or jelly used will last for an eighteen-hour period. If you have intercourse after eighteen hours, the cream or jelly will not kill sperm effectively.

If you have intercourse seventeen or eighteen hours after you insert the diaphragm, you must still wait at least six hours before you remove it. This is to make sure no live sperm are in the vagina when the diaphragm is removed. Some women prefer to leave it in place as many as twelve hours.

Be sure not to douche while the diaphragm is in place. The jet of water could force sperm around the rim of the diaphragm or wash away the protective cream or jelly. If you like to have sex in the bathtub or pool, this is not the method for you!

After removal, the diaphragm should be washed in mild soap and water, rinsed in clear water, and dried. If a woman wishes to powder it, she should not use baby powder or other body powders. These contain oils and other medications which can damage the rubber. Use cornstarch. Store the diaphragm away from heat in the plastic case that came with it.

(Check it periodically for even the tiniest hole, by holding it in front of a bright light and stretching the rubber with your fingers. Each diaphragm should last two years with proper care and should remain entirely comfortable to the woman and her partner. If it isn't, see a women's health care specialist or physician knowledgeable about diaphragms.)

Ovulation can occur at any time in a woman's monthly cycle so there is absolutely no safe time to have intercourse without your diaphragm and contraceptive cream. Although it's not common, ovulation can even occur during menstruation. Some women experience bleeding at the time of ovulation, which they may misinterpret as menstruation. It is caused by the ovum breaking through the ovary, rupturing small blood vessels there.

During menstruation or bleeding due to ovulation, the diaphragm not only gives contraceptive protection but serves to hold back the flow of blood. For the many people who are uncomfortable about intercourse during menstruation, this is an added benefit. There is no harm done if the diaphragm gets too full, for the blood merely overflows into the vagina as usual.

Missing a menstrual period does not necessarily mean a woman is pregnant, so missing a period is no reason to stop using the diaphragm. She should not assume she is pregnant until a pregnancy test shows that she is.

There are few women who cannot use the diaphragm. In some women the pelvic muscles which form the pelvic floor are not strong enough to hold the diaphragm in place if she has had many children or is overweight and out of shape. Also, if a woman has an unusually small cervix, the diaphragm will not fit properly. It is rare, but possible, to be allergic to the rubber of which the diaphragm is made. The rare woman whose skin is sensitive to spermicidal cream or jelly can usually correct the situation by changing brands.

The major objection is that inserting a diaphragm interferes with the spontaneity of sex. If you can anticipate sex, insert it beforehand. If not, you need to work it out with your partner. When a couple decides not to have children, it is a joint decision, and following through with that decision needs joint effort.

Another objection to the diaphragm is that it may be displaced during intercourse because the vagina expands with sexual excitement. The danger of this happening increases with repeated intercourse in those positions where the woman is on top. A final objection is that for some women, touching their genitals is simply out of the question and so this method is automatically ruled out for them.

Among the effective types of birth control, the diaphragm and the condom have the fewest side effects, in fact almost none. There are no hormones to worry about as there are with the pill and there is no irritation such as the IUD may cause. The woman uses the diaphragm only as needed, unlike birth control pills which are taken daily, whether or not she needs them. For many women, being in complete control of contraception this way is very attractive. For them, insertion is a very positive statement that they want to have sex, and that they care enough about themselves to prevent an unwanted pregnancy.

THE CONDOM

The condom has had rough going as a respectable contraceptive in the United States. The Comstock Act of 1873 declared it, as well as other contraceptive materials and information, obscene and therefore illegal. A black market in condom manufacture and distribution sprang up among manufacturers who had little concern for the quality of their product since it was outside the law. Thus began the bad reputation the condom has acquired.

The restriction against using the U.S. Postal Service to distribute condoms was skirted by defining them as "disease prophylactics" and that label has misled people about their potential as a contraceptive in the United States. Outdated laws in many states of the U.S. even now restrict the sale, advertising, display, or distribution of condoms. These laws underscore the association of the condom with illicit sex and disease of decades ago rather than promote the benefits the condom offers many people.

In contrast, more than two-thirds of the Japanese people who use contraceptives choose condoms as their primary technique because oral contraceptives and IUDs are illegal. Sweden has many boutiques called Flowers and Bees which have been opened by the Association for Sex Education. The cartoon symbol of "Black Jack" brand condoms is printed on T-shirts in that country.

There have been some significant changes in the U.S., though. Zero Population Growth in Seattle, Washington, for example, has opened a contraceptive boutique called "The Rubber Tree." It sells nonprescription contraceptives and offers complete information on their use and effectiveness.

Unfortunately, most physicians and researchers in the field of contraception don't promote the condom. Perhaps they, too, have fallen prey to its past association with venereal disease or feel it cannot be improved upon. On the contrary, it can be improved. Condoms made in the U.S. are the thickest in the world. This is the major objection to the condom here: it decreases sensitivity. As the saying goes, it's like taking a shower with a raincoat on. There is a similar attitude toward the diaphragm. True, neither of these methods is terribly complicated, nor intellectually challenging but each is completely safe for bodies. There are no hormones, they cannot get lost in the body, and they do not result in infections or excess bleeding. Active medical and drug company support would change people's attitudes toward the desirability of both, could be instrumental in getting quality controls changed, and could help eliminate the major objection to the condom.

In a technological age we automatically look to the newest and most sophisticated products and can lose perspective on the trade-offs that go with technology. In view of the defense it gives against sexually transmitted diseases, this old standby deserves reconsideration as an alternative contraceptive.

The condom, also called a prophylactic, rubber, safety, sheath, and skin, is one of the oldest methods of birth control known. The first description of a condom appeared in I564 when an Italian anatomist named Fallopius recommended a linen sheath moistened with a lotion as a guard against venereal disease. Its effectiveness as a contraceptive was discovered later. The linen sheath was replaced by sheep membrane which was too expensive for all but the wealthy. The first rubber condoms were made in the I870s and modern processing began in the I930s with the production of concentrated liquid natural rubber latex, the basic ingredient of modern condoms.

The technology used today to insure high quality includes electronic tests for pinholes the naked eye could never see. In a second test, condoms are filled with a certain amount of air or water to see if they burst. Better packaging and sealing techniques, including a recommended expiration date stamp, now protect the quality of the condom.

Though outdated studies quoted again and again have left the impression that the condom is a poor performer, quality testing, particularly in the U.S.. is so strict that a condom will rarely break. Failure of this method, like failure of the diaphragm, is far more likely to come from the user than the product (just as more auto accidents are caused by driver error than mechanical failure).

The condom acts as a barrier to keep sperm from getting into the vagina. When used properly, *with every act of intercourse,* the condom is highly effective. If used with foam, effectiveness is like that of combined oral contraceptives. These two provide a back-up system for each other if one method fails. However, human error is not uncommon with all things sexual. To be effective, this method needs a well-motivated man.

Proper use begins with squeezing the end of the condom to eliminate air. Then, the condom is unrolled over the erect penis *before* intercourse begins. If you are not circumcised, pull the foreskin back completely before you put on the condom.

Put the condom on before you have intercourse—don't kid yourself or your partner about putting it on before you ejaculate. This is half-safe contraception and eliminates any defense against a sexually transmitted disease.

Some types of condoms are made with a reservoir tip which collects the semen. This type of condom is recommended because when there is no space for the semen inside the condom, it can break or semen can ooze past the rim of the condom at the base of the penis and come in contact with the vagina. If you are using a condom without the nipple tip, leave a half-inch space (without air) at the tip when you put it on.

After intercourse, the penis must be withdrawn from the vagina before an erection is lost or the condom can easily slip off, canceling the contraceptive protection. If it does slip off or tear in the vagina, insert contraceptive foam or jelly immediately. And if that is not available, you have to consider the increased risk of pregnancy. During withdrawal, hold the rim or base of the condom so it does not slip off. Use a new condom *each* time intercourse is repeated and if intimate contact is continued after intercourse, wash the penis. This is more fun if the partners do it together.

In cultures where the condom is used extensively, unrolling it onto the penis is an erotic part of lovemaking rather than an irritating interruption. New shapes which contour the penis, a variety of colors (such as black, red, and green), and varied surface textures to increase sensation to the woman have been devised to make the condom more acceptable. If you want to cut down on friction and prevent tearing of the condom, lubrication helps but don't use petroleum jelly; it deteriorates the rubber. K-Y jelly, a contraceptive cream or jelly, or lubricated condoms can be used. If you're in the woods with only your partner and a condom, don't forget the old standby— saliva. Lubricated condoms are available which are either moist or treated with semi-dry silicone. Even though condoms are packaged well, don't carry condoms in a wallet or any other place next to the body for any length of time because body heat, or any kind of heat, damages the rubber. If kept away from heat, the shelf life of condoms is two years.

Cost of a single condom varies depending on the material and manufacturing process used. Condoms made from animal membranes are the most expensive, but they are coveted because they minimize the loss of sensation. These skin condoms are considered a luxury and are made only in the U.S. Yes, only in America. The rare man who is sensitive to rubber can try this type. All types can be purchased without a prescription at drugstores.

The condom offers the best protection against sexually transmitted diseases. If a person has a number of sex partners, the chance of getting a sexually transmitted disease increases. It is nearly impossible for a man to tell if his partner has one. Often he doesn't know he has one himself until the symptoms show up, and a man or a woman can be a carrier without symptoms. Use condoms if you or your partner is being treated for a sexually transmitted disease.

Other good times to use the condom are when a woman does not have a contraceptive method or drugstores are closed and she is out of cream or jelly for her diaphragm; when she has just had a child and has not resumed a method of birth control; or when she has skipped a day or two of pills and might not be protected for the rest of the month, and if the man likes to be in control. In addition, it gives visual reassurance of successful contraception.

Sex counselors recommend condoms for men having problems with premature ejaculation. The condoms are also suggested for men who have difficulty in keeping an erection until orgasm as there might be a slight tourniquet effect created by the rim of the condom at the base of the penis.

VAGINAL CONTRACEPTIVES

Vaginal contraceptives will never be as popular as the birth control pill or the IUD, but they are an important part of contraception, especially when used with the diaphragm.

They have their advantages. The fact that they can be purchased without a prescription is in their favor, particularly for younger people who don't want their family physician or parents to know they are having sexual encounters. They can be used for short-term birth control while a woman is nursing a baby and the pill would interfere with milk production. They are convenient when you are waiting to have your period in order for an IUD to be inserted, after the removal of an IUD, if you have skipped several birth control pills, or during menopause when ovulation is irregular and lubrication is welcomed. The possibility that using vaginal contraceptives lowers the number of microorganisms responsible for sexually transmitted diseases is also a plus.

The chief complaints against vaginal contraceptives are that using them interrupts the sexual engagement—they must be reinserted for each intercourse, must be inserted high into the vagina, and are expensive if used frequently.

This form of contraception has a venerable history. Egyptians were known to insert such mixtures as honey, sodium carbonate, and crocodile dung into the vagina to prevent conception. Aristotle's prescription was oil of cedar and frankincense in olive oil to stop sperm from entering the cervix. Other potions followed, such as cedar gum, different fruit acids, and astringents. Some of these probably killed some sperm and, in the case of crocodile dung, may have kept away both sperm and men.

It has been known for some time that changing the environment of the vagina to a more acid condition or a more alkaline one will effectively kill sperm. More modern improvisations and drive-in movie remedies include sponges dipped in diluted lemon juice, tampons with mustard oil, and douches of Coca-Cola—none of them good ideas.

The serious, effective, tested, and certified vaginal contraceptives are foams, creams, jellies, vaginal suppositories (tablets which melt in the vagina), and the newest contraceptive films—thin soluble sheets coated with spermicide. They can all be purchased without a prescription. The foams come in aerosol cans, and the creams and jellies in tubes. Do not confuse the contraceptive suppositories with "feminine deodorant" suppositories which do not prevent pregnancy.

All these preparations combine an inactive and an active ingredient. The inactive portion melts or foams to spread the cream, jelly, foam, or film over the upper part of the vagina and cervix. The active part is the spermicide. The two work together to prevent sperm from entering the cervix: sperm cannot swim through the inactive material and the spermicide kills them.

As with the condom and the diaphragm, human error accounts for most failures with this method and it is best used by people who are highly motivated. The failures of the method itself are low, but in a real situation where the foam or gel is left in place too long before intercourse or is not used "just this once," failure rates are very high. Research by Masters and Johnson shows that aerosol foams or creams spread more effectively over the upper vagina than creams or jellies in tubes, covering the area more thoroughly with spermicide.

If enough contraceptive is used *every* time intercourse occurs and applied again if intercourse is repeated, it is estimated that five or less women out of 100 will become pregnant after one year's use. However, there are a number of mistakes to watch for using this method. One of the most common mistakes is not having an extra bottle or tube on hand in case you run out. Other mistakes include not shaking the can of foam to mix the spermicide evenly, failing to use the contraceptive because it interrupts lovemaking, or not using enough foam. Women should use at least two applicators full of foam each time they make love.

Standing up and walking around after applying the contraceptive is a poor idea. It is okay after intercourse, but if a woman walks around beforehand, the contraceptive will run out the vagina. (If you like to have sex standing up, this is not the method for you!)

Do *not* douche until eight hours after the last intercourse. Douching is really unnecessary because the contraceptive will drain out of the vagina on its own.

All these mistakes decrease the effectiveness of foam, cream, jelly, suppositories, and films—causing about fifteen to twenty-five pregnancies for each hundred women using the method for one year.

With foam, be sure to shake the container well before use—at least twenty times—to mix the spermicide evenly throughout the foam. Follow the instructions that come with the bottle of foam and applicator and make sure the applicator is full before inserting it into the vagina.

Lie down, put the foam-filled applicator into the vagina as far as it will go (this places it underneath the cervix) and then pull it back slightly, about half an inch. Press the plunger down until the applicator is empty and remove it while holding the plunger down. Now insert another full applicator of foam.

Inserting the contraceptive too far in advance of intercourse will cause failures. It usually has to be inserted not more than fifteen to thirty minutes before intercourse, depending on the kind being used. If more time passes then put in another full applicator.

Most of these directions apply to creams and jellies too, except for the shaking part. With your finger or your partner's, place suppositories and films high in the vagina. Using the penis to place films into the vagina is a poor idea. Put foam, cream, or jellies into the vagina no sooner than fifteen minutes before intercourse. Use more foam, or whatever, each time you have sex. After intercourse it is no longer effective. At least one manufacturer has prefilled applicators that can be kept handy each time you have sex.

If the contraceptive irritates the skin of either person, try changing brands. There is reliable evidence that spermicides have an unpleasant taste. If you wish to have oral-genital sex, do it before using any sort of spermicide. If a woman needs to get out of bed right after intercourse, she can insert a tampon into the vagina to avoid the mess of semen and foam running out.

Vaginal contraceptives are invaluable when used with other methods of birth control such as the diaphragm and condom, and during mid-cycle with an IUD as is recommended by some health care specialists. When vaginal contraceptives are used with a condom, protection from pregnancy becomes nearly complete.

CONTRACEPTION WITHOUT CONTRACEPTIVES

There are several methods that both men and women have traditionally used to prevent conception but they are methods with a failure rate high enough to make them impractical for people serious about practicing contraception. These "non-methods" have a small advantage over no contraception at all but they are poor substitutes for the more effective means discussed previously.

The three methods available to women are based on fertile days. All of them require rather long periods of abstinence—no intercourse and intimate contact. All are acceptable to the Roman Catholic Church.

The temperature method and the calendar, or rhythm, methods have been in use for decades. The ovulation method has been recently introduced and has been promoted as more effective but it relies heavily on personal interpretation, individual confidence and adequate training in addition to periodic abstinence.

The one thing missing from these methods is an exact advance indicator of the day of ovulation. It has been noted that there is pain associated with ovulation but this is not experienced by all women. There are changes in the cells of the vagina but a microscope is needed to note them so it is not very practical. Ovulation can be detected by way of the urine as well as the blood, but such tests give no advance warning of ovulation. There is a change in the type and amount of mucus produced by the glands of the cervix just prior to ovulation which might prove to be a valuable indicator, yet not all women experience distinct changes.

The first method based on avoiding fertile days is the basal body temperature method (BBT). This practice began when the first descriptions of changing temperature associated with the menstrual cycle were made by Mary Jacoby in the United States in 1876. In 1905 a Dutch physician named Van de Velde suggested that ovulation occurs when the body temperature, taken upon awakening, is lowest, and there is intermenstrual pain. Unfortunately, his findings were not confirmed until thirty years later.

Ovulation occurs one or two days before a temperature rise or during the lowest temperature period, so in the strict temperature method a couple must abstain from intercourse from the menstrual period to the third day after the initial rise in temperature.

If these long periods of abstinence are unacceptable to a couple, they can chart the daily temperature for at least six cycles. The temperature is taken orally, vaginally, or rectally each morning upon awakening, before the woman gets out of bed, always at the same time, and before any activity. Because the temperature rise is slight (.5 to 1.0 degrees Fahrenheit or .3 to .5 degrees centigrade), special BBT thermometers with expanded scales and charts have been developed. A woman must take great care in reading her temperature and plot the readings on a graph.

After charting six cycles, deduct six days from the day of these cycles that shows the earliest rise in temperature. From the menstrual period to this day, which is six days before the earliest rise in temperature, a couple can have intercourse. There is, of course, no guarantee that ovulation will not occur during this time. And since the clue, the rise in temperature, occurs after ovulation, it gives no warning in advance of ovulation. Yet if it is the only method available that is acceptable to the couple, it is a reasonable calculation.

There are several errors that can occur in this method. There may be a false temperature rise, due to a cold, flu, infection, emotional tension, lack of sleep, or even an electric blanket. If the temperature is not taken every day upon awakening (before getting out of bed!) an incomplete measurement of temperature can lead to an error in charting the rise of temperature and pregnancy can result.

For young women, women approaching menopause, or women who have recently gone through childbirth or abortion, the BBT method is often impractical due to menstrual irregularity and lack of ovulation altogether. The only recourse for them is another form of contraception or abstinence until regularity has been established.

Long periods of abstinence are difficult for couples to maintain and sexual intercourse during fertile days is the most common cause of an unwanted pregnancy.

The second method based on avoiding fertile days is the calendar, or rhythm method. It, like the temperature method, uses the principle that there are more infertile days in a woman's reproductive years than there are fertile. During the fertile or "unsafe" period, intercourse is avoided. The catch is figuring out which days are unsafe.

Rhythm is defined as the recurrence or repetition of something, and in this case it is ovulation (or abstinence, depending on your point of view). Each cycle is based on the release of an ovum from one of the ovaries and it is this event that one tries to predict in the rhythm method. According to a book entitled *Science and the Safe Period*, by C. G. Hartman, the fertile or unsafe period consists of four days. Three days occur before ovulation, due to the fact of sperm survival, and one day follows ovulation, due to the survival of the ovum for twenty-four hours. The ongoing problem for scientists as well as couples using this method is: which four days?

It is known that if you take the first day of menstruation and *count back* fourteen days—give or take two days—that will be the day of ovulation. So what is needed is hindsight in order to predict on which day the egg pops out of the ovary. People not having this hindsight can end up as parents.

In order to pinpoint her unsafe days a woman needs to make a chart for several cycles so there is a visual record. If she is regular, charting cycles for a long time is not necessary. However, if the length of time between periods changes, charting cycles for as much as one year may be necessary. The greater the variation in cycle length, the longer the observation needed.

If the cycle is always twenty-eight days, then ovulation will occur between day twelve (fourteen minus two days) and day sixteen (fourteen plus two days). Leave two days more at the beginning of this interval to allow for the survival of sperm, which live for about forty-eight hours, and leave one day at the end of this interval to allow for the survival of the ovum. Sperm are capable of fertilizing an egg or ovum two days after ejaculation. So, there is an interval from day ten to day seventeen when intercourse and all intimate contact must be avoided.

If a woman does not have a twenty-eight-day cycle, the period of observation may need to last as much as one year. Then, to decide your unsafe days, first, take the shortest cycle and subtract eighteen days. (Remember fourteen plus two days plus two more days for sperm survival equals eighteen.) This will indicate the start of the fertile or unsafe period. Then, take the longest cycle and subtract eleven days and this will give the end of the fertile period:

Shortest Cycle = 26 days	Longest Cycle = 37 days
26	37
−18	−11
8th day (beginning of fertile period)	26th day (end of fertile period)

If a woman does not wish to become pregnant, she must avoid intercourse between day eight and day twenty-six of *each* cycle according to this sample.

There certainly are problems with this method. Though the rhythm method has been claimed to be absolutely safe, almost all women will menstruate up to one week early or one week late during their reproductive years. Also, most women have some cycles in which ovulation does not occur and then it can occur at any time during the next cycle, *even during menstruation*. Therefore, there is no time during the menstrual cycle that is 100% safe.

There are also risks of fertilizing an "overripe" egg. After an egg has been released it should be fertilized as soon as possible or, in other words, while it is "fresh." If the time of ovulation is incorrectly predicted, a couple has a greater chance of conception with a sperm which is not fresh or an egg which is not fresh. If the egg or sperm is "old," the possibility of developmental defects increases. The life span of an egg is twenty-four hours and the life span of a sperm is about forty-eight hours. At the end of either the twenty-four or forty-eight hour life spans, these cells begin to fall apart. If fertilization occurs at this time, the chance of mistakes in development is greater due to the lack of "freshness" of these sex cells.

The ovulation method has only recently been introduced into the United States but has been and is being used in other countries where religious beliefs are in conflict with existing contraceptive devices or pill taking. It can be used to increase the effectiveness of other methods such as the rhythm method or the basal body temperature method, and it can be used by those couples who are using barrier methods such as the diaphragm, condom, or foam. The ovulation method can alert

the couple to highly fertile days so that extra care and attention can be given to contraception.

Since fertility depends on ovulation and the life of a sperm
cell, the sperm cell must reach the site of fertilization in the
uterine tube and be healthy when it gets there. There is strong
evidence that the opening of the uterus, the cervix, must be
filled with a particular type of mucus in order for sperm to
pass. If the mucus is of the "wrong" type, the sperm cannot
pass into the uterus. If the type and amount of the mucus
change during ovulation, couldn't a woman use this information to predict when ovulation occurred?

The ovulation method involves determining the fertile days
by the type of cervical mucus which comes from the glands of
the cervix. This mucus increases in amount and becomes less
dense when a woman is fertile. It signals the approach of
ovulation.

Observation of the cervical mucus as the only guide to
periodic abstinence was first recommended in 1964 by Drs.
John and Evelyn Billings, a husband and wife team from
Australia. This method has been taught since the 1950s to
be used in combination with the temperature and calendar
methods.

It must be said that not all women experience definite
mucus symptoms and this method would not work for them.
Furthermore, as reported by *Population Reports* from George
Washington University Medical Center, there is no evidence, to
date, that the relationship between peak mucus symptoms and
ovulation is constant enough to predict ovulation in time nor
is there evidence that these symptoms can be correctly determined. The first scientific study of this method, funded by
the federal government, has begun in Los Angeles, however,
to determine the effectiveness of taking the vaginal tempera-

ture plus observing certain symptoms and using the ovulation method.

The changes in cervical mucus occur as the surface cells of the cervix make a different type of mucus in response to changes in hormone levels in the body. The changes are gradual, but can be divided into five phases.

First come the "dry days" immediately following menstruation, during which low estrogen levels fail to stimulate secretion. Second come the early preovulatory days during which estrogen levels begin to rise and stimulate secretion of a cloudy yellow or white discharge of sticky consistency. Third are the "wet days" immediately before and after ovulation, during which estrogen levels reach their peak. The cervical discharge increases, becoming clear and highly lubricative, like egg white. This is most noticeable at the time of ovulation and usually lasts one to three days afterwards. In the fourth phase, the postovulatory days, progesterone levels rise and the mucus decreases sharply, becoming cloudy and sticky. In the last, late postovulatory or immediate premenstrual phase, mucal flow may again become clear and watery. This stage does not always occur and its significance is unknown.

Women who are considering this method should search out a local person familiar with teaching it. Individual instruction has a great deal to do with the success of this method.

The ovulation, rhythm, and temperature methods all depend on the woman taking responsibility for preventing pregnancy. There are three kinds of male-controlled contraception as well, which depend on the male preventing the entrance of semen into the vagina during intercourse: coitus interruptus, coitus reservatus, and coitus obstructus.

Coitus interruptus is by far the oldest and most common method of contraception in the world. The man withdraws his penis from the vagina and vaginal area just before his orgasm and ejaculates outside of, and away from, the vagina. It costs nothing, it can't be forgotten when the couple goes away from home, the children can't find it, the government can't tax it, and it requires no medical supervision.

One disadvantage of this technique is its limited effectiveness. Pregnancy may result because sperm can enter the vagina in several ways. Some men ejaculate in stages or withdraw after some sperm have been released in the vagina. It is also possible for a small amount of sperm to be released in the lubricant secreted from the penis before and during intercourse, particularly if the man just recently ejaculated. This crystal clear fluid both clears the urethra of urine and semen and serves as a lubricant so the thick semen can slide along easily. Actual sperm counts of this clear fluid have not been published.

Some men fail to withdraw in time due to carelessness or lack of ability to predict time of ejaculation, in some cases due to the influence of alcohol or fatigue. Ejaculation near the woman's external sexual organs can permit sperm to migrate into the vagina after intercourse is completed. In men who aren't circumcised, sperm from a previous ejaculation can remain alive under the foreskin and enter the vagina later in an act of intercourse.

Apart from its liabilities as a contraceptive method, coitus interruptus is questioned by many physicians and psychologists because of its psychic and physical effects on both partners. The woman may experience anxiety during intercourse, because she cannot be sure her partner has sufficient control to withdraw in time, or she may fail to attain orgasm by the time her partner must withdraw. Men also experience anxiety over their own control and perhaps feel cheated of the full pleasure of an orgasm within the vagina.

There are two related techniques, neither of which is recommended as effective or rewarding. Coitus reservatus is a method in which the male maintains an erection until his partner has an orgasm and then withdraws without having ejaculated. The second technique, coitus obstructus, calls for firm pressure with fingers at the base of the penis at the moment of ejaculation, channeling the semen into the man's bladder rather than into his partner's vagina.

AFTER THE FACT

As soon as it was realized that semen was in some way responsible for a woman becoming pregnant, all sorts of elaborate as well as simple methods were employed to destroy semen or remove it from the vagina as quickly as possible after intercourse.

Ancient folk methods were not only ineffective but amusing. As Norman Himes in *Medical History of Contraception* writes, Soranos (98-138 A.D.) recommended that:

> . . . the woman ought, in the moment during coitus when the man ejaculated his sperm, to hold her breath, draw her body back a little so that the semen cannot penetrate into the os uteri, then immediately get up and sit down with bent knees, and, in this position, provoke sneezes. She should then wipe out the vagina carefully or drink cold water in addition.

Later a Persian physician suggested a similar method:

> First, immediately after ejaculation, let the two come apart and let the woman arise roughly, sneeze and blow her nose several times, and call out in a loud voice. She should jump violently backward seven to nine times.

The violent jumping backward was supposed to shake out the semen from the vagina, while jumping forward would assure pregnancy.

After unprotected intercourse there are several last-ditch efforts that can prevent implantation of a fertilized egg. Most are much better than sneezing. They include the morning-after treatment, insertion of an IUD, and douching. Douching is an ancient method that attempts to wash away semen; the morning-after treatment is a large dosage of estrogen that prevents implantation of the fertilized egg.

The least effective of all these "after the fact" methods is douching. It is accomplished by flushing out the vagina with some commercially prepared liquid or a solution, such as hot or cold water, in which two tablespoons of vinegar or lemon juice have been dissolved. To be useful at all, douching must be carried out immediately after intercourse. However, estimates are that sperm make their way into the uterus within ninety seconds after ejaculation, and once the sperm are in the uterus, they cannot be washed away. Therefore, the effectiveness of douching as a contraceptive is so low as to make it useless.

In fact, it can actually have the opposite effect: the pressure of the liquid may force sperm into the opening of the cervix. If a diaphragm or a vaginal spermicide has been used, a douche can neutralize the protective value and therefore should not be used until six to eight hours after intercourse.

The morning-after treatment is a means of preventing pregnancy after unprotected intercourse. The name implies that the best time to have treatment is the morning after unprotected intercourse. If treatment is begun no later than seventy-two hours after intercourse—the sooner the better—the treatment is highly effective in preventing pregnancy. It usually consists of taking a massive dose (a hundred times as much as a low-dosage of birth control pills) of estrogen. The name of this estrogen is diethylstilbestrol, known commonly as DES. It is taken in pills over a five-day period. An overdose of regular oral contraceptives will not have the same effect! The most common side effects of the treatment are nausea, vomiting, and general discomfort and these are most severe during the first day or two. Menstrual bleeding may begin five or eight days after all the pills have been taken.

Those risks associated with birth control pills, such as blood clotting, are present with morning-after pills. And since there are many unanswered questions about the impact of this massive dose on the body, this method is recommended only for emergency use, such as rape cases.

The treatment is not a contraceptive. It does not protect against pregnancy during treatment or during the rest of the menstrual cycle. The physical effects of repeated treatments are unknown; hence many health facilities are reluctant to give the treatment more than once to the same woman. If you are having intercourse, regularly or frequently, a regular and effective type of contraceptive should be used.

In addition to its use as a morning-after treatment, DES has been employed for other purposes. In the last several decades, for instance, it has been prescribed for menopausal women as well as for women during pregnancy. In the 1940s through the 1960s, this drug was prescribed for women during known, high-risk pregnancies to prevent miscarriages. Studies in the 1950s failed to show the benefits of this drug and in November, 1971, the U.S. Food and Drug Administration warned against its use in pregnancy due to a rare form of cancer that was found in some young women whose mothers took DES.

Every woman whose mother took DES when she was pregnant has an increased risk of developing vaginal cancer. This is because the developing fetus is infinitely sensitive to any drug taken by the mother and will absorb it in concentrated amounts. Also, the reproductive tracts of both males and females are formed during the first three months of pregnancy, making the fetus susceptible to drugs such as DES taken early in pregnancy.

Obviously, the time this drug is given is crucial. If given before implantation it works to stop implantation and is termed morning-after treatment. If given after a pregnancy has already been established, it is dangerous for the developing fetus. And if DES is given during the sixth week of pregnancy or later, the female embryo may face a higher than usual risk of developing a rare form of genital cancer later in life.

Because of the link between DES taken in the sixth week of pregnancy or later, and vaginal cancer in female offspring and genital abnormalities in males, many clinics or physicians will not prescribe morning-after treatment (MAT) to women who would choose to continue their pregnancy if MAT failed. However, there is no evidence that the MAT, when given within seventy-two hours after unprotected intercourse, will lead to genital cancer in female offspring conceived if the treatment fails.

The third means of preventing pregnancy after unprotected intercourse is insertion of a copper IUD. Because implantation takes place six or more days after fertilization, an IUD can be inserted into the uterus after coitus but before implantation. A copper IUD is chosen because the contraceptive effect of the copper begins to work soon after insertion and, also, this type is easier to insert in women who have had no pregnancies.

However, as with every other method, there are risks. Women must be carefully screened because a woman who has pelvic inflammatory disease (PID) or a sexually transmitted disease could have serious complications if an IUD is inserted.

Since tests for gonorrhea take several days to analyze, the use of an IUD as a post-coital method of birth control (without proper follow-up care) could be dangerous.

VASECTOMY

Sterilization of the male is a procedure which permanently prevents conception by that male. Couples or individuals who have decided to have no more children, or no children at all, should give vasectomy serious consideration as a contraceptive method.

It is nearly one hundred percent effective. The rare cases where pregnancy resulted after a vasectomy were mostly due to the man having intercourse without contraception immediately after the operation, when sperm were still in the reproductive tract. (A man needs periodic tests for several months after a vasectomy to establish the fact of its success.) The tubes which are severed have been known to rejoin spontaneously and reestablish fertility. And, there is at least one case on record when a woman has assumed she was protected from pregnancy with several men when in fact her husband was the only one who had had a vasectomy.

Vasectomy has its limitations, but it has its advantages. The biggest plus is that it has no physical effects on sexual enjoyment or performance in either men or women.

If a woman's health or life would be threatened by pregnancy, sterilization is a very good idea, as it is if she dislikes or fears other contraceptive methods. The financial cost of both children and contraceptives, a social awareness of overpopulation, and the human cost of unwanted pregnancies on parents, the child, and society may lead to the decision not to have children and thus to sterilization.

As far as the cost of sterilization is concerned, insurance

companies in most states, and Medicaid Insurance in many states, will cover part of the cost of vasectomy.

Sterilization can be thought of as surgical birth control. In men it is done by vasectomy; in women, by tubal ligation. Vasectomy (vas = duct and ectomy = to cut) is a simple procedure designed to block the passage of sperm through the two tubes, vasa deferentia, which carry sperm from the testicles to the urethra in the penis.

The first vasectomies were done in the late 1800s to reduce the complications of prostate operations, and for overall body rejuvenation in the early 1900s, even though it was later discovered that this did not work. National family planning programs around the world sought simple, reliable, one-time contraceptive methods and vasectomy filled that need, particularly where women refused to go to male doctors and female doctors were rare.

In the United States, adverse publicity about oral contraceptives and the IUD has led to about half a million men choosing vasectomies every year. There are millions of vasectomies done worldwide, many more than female tubal ligations. One reason for the acceptance of this method is that it is the only one with almost no risk of death. It involves fewer surgical risks than the female tubal ligation, is less costly, and takes less time.

A vasectomy can be reversed, but the chances of success are far less than perfect. It is best to consider a vasectomy as permanent.

There are many misunderstandings about vasectomies including the belief that sexual functioning will be affected. The only change after a vasectomy is the absence of sperm in the seminal fluid. One interesting fact, though, is that the level of a certain enzyme, acid phosphatase, found in semen, increases. If semen is placed under ultraviolet light, this enzyme can be detected. This kind of testing is used for medico-legal proof in rape cases.

Vasectomy does not interfere with hormones or production of the seminal fluid which is formed chiefly from the seminal vesicles and the prostate. These glands are not involved in the procedure and continue to function as before. Because sperm make up little of the volume of each ejaculation, the amount of fluid released during orgasm will be about the same.

However, the volume of fluid has not been as great a concern as the fear of impotence. The most successful vasectomies are performed on men who are individually ready, free of pressure, and understand the operation and what it will do for them.

In some cultures, the chief symbol of masculinity has been the ability to reproduce, and reluctance to accept vasectomy is common in such societies. However, in the United States much less importance is placed on the number of children a man can father as a sign of masculinity.

From start to finish the actual vasectomy operation will take from ten to thirty minutes. The man considering this procedure ordinarily will be interviewed by a physician (usually a urologist) to be sure he knows this is essentially permanent and is comfortable with the decision. If he is married it is best that both husband and wife agree to the vasectomy (or tubal ligation); in some states there are laws requiring both husband and wife to give signed permission for surgical birth control procedures. These points are not only important but vital.

The vasa deferentia are small tubes which come from the testicles. Each testicle has one tube, and the function of each is to carry sperm towards the urethra. These tubes can be reached easily by making two small incisions in the back of the scrotum, which is the loose sac of skin covering the testicles.

The incisions are made above the testicles, which are not exposed.

The area will usually be shaved and cleaned with an antiseptic solution to reduce the bacteria count. Then a local anesthetic is used to numb the area. A sedative may also be given.

A small incision is made on each side of the scrotum. The physician lifts out each vas deferens from the scrotal sac. They look like wet spaghetti. Each one is cut and sealed and sometimes a piece of tube is removed. Usually the free ends of each tube are turned away from each other or the covering tissue layer of the vas itself is pulled over the cut end. This is necessary because even if the tubes are cut, they have been known to find each other and fuse again. There are many ways the tubes can be cut and sealed. The technique selected will vary with the individual and physician doing the procedure.

After these two incisions are closed, the man should rest fifteen to thirty minutes before going home and is advised to rest for several hours once he gets home. This is a precautionary measure to avoid strain in the scrotal area. In addition, strenuous activity interferes with the healing process and so should be avoided for a few days. Some physicians suggest or require ice packs every half hour for several hours after the operation to reduce pain and swelling.

For a few days the man should wear a good, tight athletic support, and should not have intercourse. Ejaculation puts pressure on the vas deferens which can cause leakage of sperm from the cut ends. He should keep the scrotum dry for at least twenty-four hours. Additionally, heavy work should be avoided for this period of time.

There may be pain in this area after the local anesthetic wears off but this may be expected any time skin and nerve endings are cut. Also, there may be some discoloration or bruising of this area due to small blood vessels that have been broken.

Skin discoloration, swelling, and pain are the most frequent and least serious side effects of vasectomy. These reactions, though, are common to all surgery. Infection is infrequent—it is estimated that it happens in less than one percent of the procedures. Usually the infection responds to antibiotics or drainage. In rare instances, it can be serious and lead to loss of a testicle.

Another complication of vasectomy is hemorrhage into the scrotum, which may result in swelling and discomfort, but these symptoms go away on their own unless the area becomes infected. Sperm granuloma occurs rarely. This is caused by the leakage of sperm from the duct into the surrounding tissues. It is painful, and the granuloma may have to be removed surgically.

Recanalization happens in rare cases up to nine to ten months after a vasectomy. The only way to be sure rejoining of the cut ends of the vas deferens has not occurred is to check the seminal fluid for sperm periodically up to that time. If there has been a rejoining, then a repeat vasectomy is required.

Individuals or couples who are poorly prepared, inadequately motivated, or unable to accept the procedure for psychological reasons may fare badly after a vasectomy. A vasectomy is particularly unsuitable for the couple whose relationship is about to dissolve and who grasp at vasectomy as a last straw to preserve it.

Because there are still live sperm in each vas deferens between the cut portion and the urethra, the man will be fertile for several weeks after the operation. At least two consecutive ejaculations must be free of sperm to consider the man infertile. In order to accomplish this, anywhere from six to thirty-six ejaculations may be needed. It is very important that the couple use some other form of effective contraception during this period. In a month or six weeks a specimen of the seminal fluid is examined in a laboratory to determine whether it is free of sperm and another sample is taken shortly thereafter.

Sexual functioning, the experience of ejaculation, and the approximate amount of fluid that is ejaculated remain the same after a vasectomy. In fact, according to some men who have had vasectomies, their sexual life is more enjoyable because the fear of an unplanned pregnancy has been removed. The testicles continue to produce sperm but in smaller numbers. Exactly what happens to the sperm which are produced is not known as yet, but it is thought they are absorbed by the cells of the tubes and surrounding tissues behind which sperm are blocked.

Over fifty percent of all men who have had vasectomies begin to produce antibodies to their own sperm. There has been concern about these antibodies produced after vasectomy but so far it has not been proved they are harmful. Such antibodies are found in some infertile males. In addition, fertile men who have not had a vasectomy may also have similar antibodies. In fact, these antibodies may be helpful in getting rid of sperm buildup in the genital tract.

As already stated, the vasectomy should be considered permanent. Yet, when loss of children or divorce and remarriage occur some men seek to have the vasectomy reversed.

With new surgical techniques, there is a fifty percent chance that the ducts can be rejoined. Yet, this is not the only factor to be considered due to the fact that repair of the severed sperm-carrying ducts does not result in pregnancy very often. It is estimated that reversing the procedure is less than thirty percent effective in allowing fertilization. The failure is attributed to decreased production of sperm after the vasectomy, production of antibodies against the sperm that do exist, and scarring of the vas deferens (after the original surgery) that blocks sperm movement when the vasectomy is reversed.

Some men seek to store their own sperm in a sperm bank on the eve of vasectomy, so to speak, in case the time should ever arise when they want to father a child. Yes, there are real sperm banks where your sperm can be stored by freezing it in liquid nitrogen. Stored in this state, sperm are about thirty to sixty percent active and mobile after their hibernation. And caution must be advised because no studies have been done of long-term storage effects on sperm or the risks of developmental abnormalities in humans. There is at least one known case in which the fail-safe mechanism on the freezer failed and the sperm thawed.

What needs to be emphasized here is that if a man goes to these great lengths to preserve his sperm, perhaps he might question whether he really wants a vasectomy.

Several years ago there was a big splash about "on-off" valves that could be positioned along each vas deferens for a reversible method of birth control. We haven't heard much about the idea recently for the simple reason that it doesn't work. As said previously, even if the vas deferens can be opened again, there is no assurance of normal production and flow of sperm. Additionally, the technical difficulties of hooking up a valve to each vas deferens have not been overcome.

FEMALE STERILIZATION

The term "tubal ligation" could be used for cutting and sealing either the uterine tubes or the two vas deferens in the male, but it almost always refers to females.

It is a permanent, irreversible procedure that prevents the ovum and sperm from meeting by either blocking or removing a section of the uterine tubes. This procedure is over ninety-nine percent effective and does not interfere with hormone production, menstruation, menopause, or anything but pregnancy. There have been a few failures when uterine tubes rejoined after the procedure or the uterine tubes were not effectively cut or blocked by the surgery.

Because the uterine tubes are located deep inside the pelvis of the female, the task of reaching them surgically is more difficult than reaching the two vas deferens in the male, and until recent years, a simple sterilization operation for women was nonexistent. Vasectomy or male sterilization was the best minor surgical method available to couples or individuals who had completed their family or wished no children at all. But for personal and psychological reasons, vasectomy did not answer the needs of all. Yet some women who did not wish ever to become pregnant were faced with either a major operation or prolonged use of hormonal or mechanical contraception.

In 1969, the American College of Obstetricians and Gynecologists, recognizing the needs for liberalized sterilization, removed all restrictions on voluntary sterilization. They stated that voluntary sterilization was a decision between the patient and her physician, regardless of age, marital status, or number of children. This resulted in a flurry of research projects to explore surgical techniques to offer such a service to women with the same simplicity as vasectomy and at a reasonable cost. An instrument called the laparoscope was invented and the surgical method called laparoscopy was developed to perform tubal ligations and other relatively simple types of surgery inside the abdominal cavity.

Cutting and sealing the uterine tubes with the aid of a laparoscope can be done when a woman has not recently been pregnant, after pregnancy termination, and between the second and fifth days after childbirth. The main limitations to the use of this technique are the cost of the instrument and the need for a physician trained in the use of the scope. This instrument makes tubal ligation a short, safe hospital procedure that causes little or no scarring. It has become popular for a number of reasons. First, the patient is in the hospital only four to six hours. Fifty percent of the patients return to full activity in twenty-four hours. Discomfort is minimal and seldom requires pain pills stronger than aspirin. There is no noticeable scar and no restriction on intercourse.

Basically the laparoscope instrument is a slender (as big around as a fountain pen), stainless steel tube containing fiber optic bundles which transmit light but not heat through the scope into the abdominal cavity. A small incision is made just below the navel for this slender instrument so the surgeon can see the pelvic organs. A second, small incision is made below the first to introduce the instruments necessary to cut and block the uterine tubes. With the newest laparoscopes only one incision is necessary because a narrow operating channel within the slender tube allows the surgeon to see the pelvic organs and do the procedure at the same time through this channel.

The following description of a typical laparoscopic sterilization procedure will give you an idea of this method.

Anyone who has had an operation of any sort involving anesthesia will be familiar with the routine of preparing for the event. The patient readies herself for surgery in a hospital or surgical facility and she will receive a general or gas anesthetic similar to that used by dentists for dental work and tooth extractions. (Thus, she awakens quickly after the operation.) Once she is asleep, the abdomen is washed thoroughly in preparation for the surgery.

The fact that all the organs are in close proximity in the

pelvic area makes it necessary to put gas into the abdominal cavity to inflate it. This allows not only a better view of the pelvic organs with the laparoscope but makes them easier to reach because the intestines fall back from the front part of the abdominal wall. After the abdomen is inflated, a small incision, half an inch long, is made in, or just below, the navel and the laparoscope is inserted into the abdomen.

If the scope has an operating channel the uterine tubes are then manipulated in the following ways. The first method is to grasp the tube with a small surgical forcep and seal the tube in several places with electric current. The second method is to seal the tube and then cut the tube apart in one or more places. The third method combines the first two methods, but also removes a small portion of each tube.

If the scope does not have an operating channel, a second incision must be made at the level of the pubic hair line. This incision is only one quarter of an inch long and does not alter the recovery rate of the patient. In fact, many patients don't even notice it.

Once the operation is completed, the gas is removed from the abdominal cavity and the instruments removed. Hidden dissolving stitches are usually used to suture the incision. A band-aid is applied and the patient is sent to the recovery room. After one to three hours she is sent home with instructions not to drive for twenty-four to forty-eight hours and to rest as necessary. (Some women have been able to go out to dinner that evening!) Most physicians request the patient to return in two or three weeks for a follow-up exam. Whereas vasectomy is not effective for two months, tubal sterilization is effective immediately.

There is still no surgical sterilization method invented that is one hundred percent guaranteed. (In fact, ten women in recorded medical history have become pregnant after a hysterectomy.) The most common reason for failure of tubal ligation is that the woman is already pregnant at the time of the procedure. In general, the skill of the surgeon, more than any other single factor, determines the success and safety of a tubal ligation.

This procedure is not recommended for women with severe heart or lung disorders, hernia, previous abdominal surgery (specifically scarring and/or adhesions), obesity, or pelvic inflammatory disease (PID).

The more traditional method of tubal ligation is usually performed within forty-eight hours after childbirth. At this time the uterine tubes are easiest to tie; they are near the surface of the abdominal wall just under the stretched skin of the surface.

If the mother and baby are in good condition, a tubal ligation can be done immediately after delivery. A small incision is made just below the navel and the tubes are located. A small portion of each tube is removed and the free ends are tied shut with stitches. Each tube can also be squeezed shut with a clip. The incision is then closed. This procedure takes about twenty minutes and it can be performed by any physician with general surgical training without the need for specialized instruments.

The same anesthetic, either general or local, that is used for childbirth can often be used for the tubal ligation procedure. There is little pain afterwards. The hospital stay is usually not any longer than that required for delivery—usually about three days, particularly when the procedure is done immediately after childbirth. Of course, if the woman wishes to deliver at home she will need to be hospitalized specifically for this procedure. Estimates of complications due to infection or bleeding range from two to four percent.

Another version of tubal ligation is done independently of

childbirth when a laparoscopy or an approach through the vagina is not medically advisable. In addition, this procedure might be done when an incision in the abdomen is necessary for another reason, for example, an appendectomy. The incision is somewhat larger than the one used just after childbirth and, accordingly, postoperative discomfort is greater. A small portion of each tube is removed in the same manner as after childbirth. A general anesthetic is used and the hospital stay is usually several days. Infections associated with the incision are the major complications but if the procedure is done properly, such infections are uncommon.

There is another variation of traditional tubal ligation called minilaparotomy. The result is the same, but the procedure differs. The technique can be used after childbirth or when a woman has not recently been pregnant.

A small incision is made at the pubic hairline. The uterus is maneuvered to bring the uterine tubes into view. A portion of each tube is brought through the small incision and the tubes are tied or sealed in some fashion. No special training or expensive equipment is needed with this technique in contrast to laparoscopic tubal ligation. Yet, like laparoscopic tubal ligation, there is little or no scar visible since the pubic hair camouflages the area.

Since only a small incision is necessary, local anesthetic can be used but often general or spinal anesthesia is used in the United States. The procedure can be done on an outpatient basis for women who have not recently been pregnant. It takes ten to thirty minutes to perform. In addition, the small incision is less traumatic for the woman.

The incision should be kept dry and clean; the stitches are removed about a week after the operation. The woman can have intercourse as soon as she likes.

As with other sterilization methods, there are women who

should not have this operation. If they are obese or have abdominal adhesions, pelvic inflammatory disease (PID), or a uterus which cannot be moved easily, this is not for them.

And, finally, there is a procedure for tubal ligation that approaches through the vagina. Sometimes it is performed after an abortion that has been done within the first twelve weeks of pregnancy. Vaginal tubal ligation can be done in ten or fifteen minutes but should be done by a physician trained in gynecology.

Although incisions made with the laparoscopic method are very small, some women find the vaginal technique more attractive because there is no visible external incision. Due to possible infection, and the need for the incision to heal, though, intercourse is prohibited for up to six weeks with this method.

The operation begins with an incision deep in the vagina, just behind the cervix. The tubes are brought close to the vaginal incision (by moving the uterus), grasped, and pulled down into the vagina. A loop is made in each tube, secured with stitches, and the top of the looped portion is removed. The vaginal incision is then closed.

Another technique, after the incision in the vagina is made, is to remove the ends of the uterine tubes. This is called a fimbriectomy. The entire procedure takes from five to fifteen minutes and minimum preparation includes routine lab tests, pelvic exam, and cleansing of the vagina and vulva.

The anesthetic can be general, local, or spinal. In the United States vaginal sterilizations are usually done under general anesthesia. Plan on at least overnight in the hospital and perhaps several days, depending on your rate of recovery.

Infection is the most common postoperative complication of a vaginal tubal ligation. Since bacteria are a natural part of the vagina, it is difficult to achieve a sterile environment surgically. The absence of complications may depend on how long intercourse is postponed following surgery. The first indication of infection will be a fever. When vaginal tubal ligation is performed after a termination of pregnancy or other procedure, there is a higher rate of complications.

A hysterectomy is sometimes suggested as a means of sterilization and, until recently, was the most common method of permanent contraception.

A hysterectomy is the removal of the uterus. The word "hystero" has a Greek origin and it means womb. Hysteria was once thought to be caused by disturbances in the womb. We have been stuck with the word since.

Some people feel a hysterectomy is a drastic method of sterilization, which removes an organ that is important to a woman's self-esteem and sense of female identity. And recently, researchers in human sexual response, namely Masters and Johnson, have argued that the uterus is an important part of the female orgasmic response in some women.

Some physicians have compared the uterus to a baby carriage which serves no other purpose, and, they say, after no more children are desired it should be eliminated. In considering these two sides of the coin, it should be noted that this operation is extremely profitable for the surgeon and there is more than speculation that this single factor has had a great deal to do with the fact that hysterectomies are the most common surgical procedure performed on women in the United States. If any woman's physician is pressing her to have this operation, it might be wise for her to seek one or more medical opinions since it is major surgery and, with any major surgery, there is a risk of death.

MENOPAUSE

Menopause is the time in a woman's life when reproductive

function comes to an end. It is a perfectly normal process which usually takes from one to three years. It is not an illness and it causes no illnesses, although, coincidentally, at that age other illnesses may show up for the first time.

Menopause occurs when the ovaries reduce their hormone production despite proper stimulation from the brain centers that normally control ovarian hormone production. At the time of menopause, the ovaries gradually stop producing and liberating eggs. Ovarian hormone production gradually stops, and menstrual periods end. Ovulation is often delayed, leading to late periods. In some cycles, ovulation may not occur at all, and in these cycles menstrual bleeding may be heavier than usual.

Most women go through menopause between the ages of forty and fifty, although some women begin menopause in their late thirties, and a few continue to have regular periods and may even be fertile in their early fifties. The average age of menopause in the U. S. is forty-eight.

There is no one menopausal pattern that occurs in all women. Among the more frequent patterns are increasing length between periods, decreased menstrual flow, and gross irregularity of menstrual periods. Some women have regular periods which simply stop all of a sudden.

Any bleeding occurring between periods is definitely suspicious and should be brought to your doctor's attention immediately! Bleeding in between periods, bleeding after intercourse, heavier or longer periods each month are abnormal.

A common menopausal symptom is hot flashes. A hot flash is a feeling of warmth that suddenly spreads over the skin of the face, neck, and chest. It is often accompanied by intense perspiration. It lasts only a minute or so. The cause of the feeling of warmth is sudden dilation of the blood vessels near the surface of the skin. This is thought to stem from a disturbance in the brain centers that normally control ovarian hormone production. Since the ovaries are no longer responding to their stimulation, they try, with massive outputs of hormones, to reinstitute ovarian hormone production. Somehow, in this effort these brain centers trigger the vascular instability that is often a feature of menopause.

About eighty-five percent of all women going through menopause experience some hot flashes. In about fifteen percent of menopausal women, the symptom is severe enough to require taking estrogenic hormone. The estrogen makes the pituitary gland think the ovaries are working again. The pituitary then decreases its production of substances to make the ovaries work and the disturbance quiets down.

Headaches, insomnia, fatigue, depression, and irritability are frequently mentioned as common menopausal symptoms. All these symptoms frequently occur for other reasons and it is difficult to relate them directly to lack of estrogen. They happen more often to women who have shown some emotional instability in the past, and who have experienced similar symptoms earlier in their lives. Women who have strong interests outside the home seem to experience the least symptoms. In some women, however, these symptoms may be directly related to lack of estrogen and a prescription of estrogen gives relief quickly.

It must be kept in mind that a multitude of natural changes may be taking place in the world of the average menopausal woman, aside from the hormonal changes in her body. These include children leaving home for school or marriage and, often, a husband at the apex of his professional career while his wife suddenly finds she has nothing to do, no children to care for, and no goals for herself other than being a housewife.

Our society places a premium on physical attractiveness

for a woman, and this means youth. A man is often considered attractive on the basis of his accomplishments or his station in life. His physical attributes are a small part of his "value." It is for reasons such as these that the aging process is not as kind to a woman as it is to a man, and that menopause per se may be the scapegoat for the many other changes that occur at this time of life.

Lack of estrogen, if it is part of a woman's menopausal problems, may lead to vaginal and vulvar irritation and dryness. The skin of the vagina and vulva may become thin and dry and intercourse may be painful. Administration of estrogens, either orally or in the form of vaginal creams, will alleviate these symptoms.

For the fifteen percent of women who suffer severe menopausal symptoms, estrogen replacement is effective providing there are no medical reasons against its use. However, the FDA recommends that the lowest effective dose be used at all times, and the drug be discontinued or reduced in dosage at regular intervals to assess whether it is still needed.

For the seventy percent of women who have mild symptoms and the fifteen percent who have no symptoms at all, the question of "estrogen forever" is being answered increasingly with a "no." The Commissioner of Foods and Drugs during his testimony on estrogens stated, "It seems clear that usage of estrogens for postmenopausal symptoms is currently well beyond what many physicians would consider wise in light of the recently described association with endometrial (uterine) cancer." The association has been made between prolonged use of estrogens in postmenopausal women and the occurrence of endometrial cancer. Contrary to popular belief, estrogens will not retard the process of aging.

After menopause there is some hormone production by the adrenal glands. Some of this is estrogenic hormone and some is androgenic (masculine) hormone. The androgenic hormone may be responsible for increased facial hair growth in postmenopausal women. Most women have sufficient estrogenic hormone production to maintain skin tone, vaginal tone, lubrication, and so on.

If a woman's own hormone production is insufficient, though, and she has hot flashes, complains of dry and irritated vagina, depression, headaches, and so on, estrogen replacement will in most cases stop these symptoms. (At least it will stop the hot flashes and vaginal symptoms.)

There are, too, many diseases which first show up at the time of life in which menopause occurs. Among these are diabetes; breast, uterine, bowel, and other cancers; high blood pressure; and obesity. A yearly physical examination, including pelvic and breast exam, Pap smear (test for cancer of the cervix), blood pressure, and so on should be routine. Don't forget about a self-breast exam once a month!

"Middle-age spread" is a problem of middle age rather than specifically of menopause. It may occur well in advance of either. While it is true that some tone is lost from body tissues at the time of menopause, most of the problems of "middle-age spread" are related to lack of exercise and too much food. Fewer calories are required with increasing age to maintain constant weight.

To keep in the best possible health, a menopausal woman should check her breasts once a month, bringing any abnormalities to the immediate attention of a physician. She should watch her diet, exercise, and consult a doctor about any abnormal symptoms.

Many good studies have shown that the average couple who has had good sexual adjustment in earlier life continues to be sexually active after the woman has gone through menopause. Many women find their sexual activities are even less restricted after menopause when there is no longer the fear of pregnancy. There are no longer the limiting factors associated with young children in the house, and many women have more leisure time with fewer family responsibilities so they feel more relaxed at home. Conversely, couples who have had a poor sexual adjustment tend to limit or eliminate sexual activity at this time of life. Many well-adjusted couples continue to be sexually active well into their eighties.

There is nothing about menopause per se that suddenly stops a woman's sexual drive. Illness and processes of aging may diminish the frequency and intensity of sexual activity, but this is not specifically related to menopause.

Some form of contraception should be used for one year after the last menstrual period. If it has been one year since the last period, it can be safely assumed that ovulation has ceased permanently and pregnancy cannot occur.

When a woman is approaching her forties and has completed her family, tubal ligation is a good alternative to investigate. And since she has many times taken sole responsibility for contraception, she should ask her husband or partner if he would consider a vasectomy. Both procedures are quite safe and effective. Of course, a tubal ligation would be less appropriate if a woman was in her late forties when fertility is about to end anyway.

Whereas birth control pills have been used in the past for estrogen replacement as well as for contraception in menopausal aged women, recent evidence indicates that an increased risk of myocardial infarction (heart attack) in users of oral contraceptives exists, particularly in women forty and above. Therefore women in this age group are urged to use an alternate form of contraception.

If replacement hormones are needed, pure estrogens can be prescribed for relief of severe symptoms. Many doctors prescribe a progesterone-like hormone cyclically along with the estrogen. This means taking estrogen for the first twenty-five days of the month and taking the progesterone-like hormone during the last five days that estrogen is taken.

If an IUD has been inserted before the time of menopause, a woman can continue this method provided there are no problems with intermenstrual bleeding (bleeding between periods) or very heavy periods. If either of these occurs, it could be a symptom of a tumor or malignancy, and would have to be appropriately investigated. These symptoms are particularly worrisome in a woman of the age group predisposed to cancer of the uterus or cervix. Since many women have irregular bleeding produced by the IUD when they use it and it is impossible to rule out cancer without expensive tests, some physicians discourage the use of an IUD at the time of menopause. If a woman has an IUD at the time of menopause without any adverse symptoms, it may be left in until one year after the last menstrual period and then removed when contraception is no longer required.

The diaphragm, or foam, is entirely appropriate and highly effective for a woman in her forties and fifties. The additional lubrication from foams and gels is usually welcomed by many women who are experiencing dryness of the vagina.

Injectables are not suggested for general use.

3

ABORTION

Abortion has been, is, and will be an emotional subject. No legislation, however enlightened and necessary, will completely remove this emotional content. Hundreds of thousands—close to one million women a year seek pregnancy termination in the United States. The demand is not anything new; for centuries women have sought to terminate unwanted pregnancies, legally or illegally. Revisions in state laws and the landmark U.S. Supreme Court decision of 1973 finally made it possible for a woman to obtain a safe, legal abortion in the United States.

Although abortion is not a procedure that a woman should use as a method of contraception, it is a needed option in case a contraceptive method fails, if the people using the method fail, or if no method has been used. However, abortion presents to any woman an emotional challenge more difficult than contraception, particularly because of the emotionally charged political, moral, religious, and ethical arena in which she makes her decision. Many pregnancies are expressions of emotional needs more complicated than the immediate need an abortion can satisfy. A woman who has an abortion may experience or express uncomfortable thoughts and feelings that are perfectly normal and should not be allowed to damage her self-esteem.

All people make mistakes. If you are pregnant and don't want a child, a safe, legal abortion is available to you. Terminating a pregnancy is a choice that says, "I'm human and I make mistakes, but now I'm taking responsibility for directing my own life."

Abortion is the termination of a pregnancy after the embryo has become attached to the wall of the uterus. It is a relatively simple medical procedure when a woman is less than twelve weeks pregnant and it can be done on an out-patient basis in a clinic or private physician's office.

After the twelfth week, though, the fetal tissues are too large to be removed by simple means and a different procedure must be used to terminate pregnancy. A pregnancy termination at this time, in general, is much more traumatic.

The first step in making a decision to seek an abortion is to verify the fact that you are actually pregnant. Many physiological and emotional conditions can cause pregnancy-like symptoms. If you have missed a period, call a clinic or doctor's office and say you want a pregnancy test. If there is an urgent reason why you cannot wait to have the pregnancy confirmed, some doctors and clinics will do an early pregnancy termination one to two weeks after a missed period. In any case, it is vital that you act quickly. The farther along the pregnancy, the more involved, costly, and time consuming the procedure becomes, in addition to its possible psychological impact on you.

The Supreme Court Decision of 1973 made it possible for women to obtain safe, legal abortions. This decision was based in part on the Fourteenth Amendment concept of personal liberty being "broad enough to encompass a woman's decision whether or not to terminate her pregnancy." In 1976, the Supreme Court reaffirmed and expanded a woman's right to a legal abortion by ruling that a married woman does not need her husband's consent and an unmarried woman under eighteen does not need the consent of a parent during the first three months.

However, these decisions do not dictate that physicians or clinics have to offer this procedure and there are many women who still have difficulty in finding a doctor who will do it. If you are in a town where you feel there is no doctor or clinic that will help you, call the nearest Planned Parenthood Association or family planning clinic and tell them your situation. They can refer you to the nearest doctor or clinic that can help you. It might be necessary to travel to another town or city.

There is no safe way a woman can abort herself. There is no safe chemical that can be taken by mouth that will bring on a termination of pregnancy, nor will jumping around, horseback riding, or other violent physical activity do the job. A self-induced abortion, as with a knitting needle or coat hanger inserted into the uterus, is extremely dangerous and should *never* be attempted.

Some women may be afraid that infertility will result from a pregnancy termination. The fear stems from an era during which abortions were illegal, medical techniques were crude, and there were no antibiotics. Severe infections resulted in sterility or death. Since safe abortions have been available to women through reliable physicians, sterility is highly unusual.

The fear of pain should never prevent you from seeking early termination of pregnancy. There is absolutely no reason why a woman needs to experience discomfort. Some doctors do not use enough medication to prevent pain entirely, but if **you** are uncomfortable during the procedure, speak out!

Remember that you do not have to be punished for having sex.

There are three methods of pregnancy termination in use at this time. Two of them can be performed within fourteen weeks after the last menstrual period (the first trimester of pregnancy). The third one is done between fourteen and twenty-four weeks (the second trimester), and in some cases is also used in the third trimester when the life or the health of the mother is at stake.

Over 90% of pregnancy terminations in the United States are done by a suction method of dilation and curettage (D & C) in the first twelve to fourteen weeks of pregnancy. (Twelve to fourteen from the last menstrual period)

This procedure was first outlined by a Russian physician in 1927. In the 1950s Chinese physicians, followed by the Soviet Union, Eastern Europe, the United Kingdom, and finally the United States, adopted this method. Abortion reform laws were passed in the states of New York, California, Washington, Hawaii, and Alaska, followed by the Supreme Court decision of 1973. As pointed out in *Progress in Gynecology*, "the well-documented safety record for outpatient abortions has encouraged the growth of many specialized abortion clinics in the United States. Such centers can provide group support, counseling on abortion and contraception, and abortion care by a well-trained physician at a lower cost and in a more reassuring, informal atmosphere than the hospital operating room."

When you go to the doctor you have chosen, a medical history will be taken. Many times counseling on your feelings about pregnancy termination and future contraceptive plans will be done at this time. If there are any questions on the procedure or what method of birth control you would like to use in the future, don't hesitate to ask. The fact that you are being offered a safe, legal pregnancy termination indicates, in the majority of situations, that your needs will be understood.

A pelvic exam will be done to determine the number of weeks of pregnancy and any abnormalities of the reproductive tract. It is particularly important to be sure a woman does not have a sexually transmitted disease or other infection at this time. If she does have an infection, this is treated with anti-biotics before the abortion is done.

A positive pregnancy test is usually required. In addition, blood testing is necessary to check for anemia and to deter-mine whether your blood is Rh positive or negative. If your blood is Rh negative, then an immune globulin shot will be required shortly after the pregnancy termination. This shot is needed after each and every pregnancy, when Rh blood factors are in conflict, whether or not you terminate the pregnancy early or carry to full term.

Most physicians give a sedative to the woman either in the form of a pill or by injection before the procedure.

A suction D & C is done while the woman lies on her back, legs apart, knees bent, and feet supported by metal stirrups just as in the pelvic exam. A speculum is placed in the vagina so the cervix can easily be seen. Then a local anesthetic is injected into the cervix.

A laminaria tent may have been used to widen the cervical canal. It is a sea-grown plant capable of soaking up fluids from the cervical canal. This plant is dried and formed into a long narrow tube, sterilized, and inserted into the opening of the uterus the day before termination of pregnancy. This tech-nique for softening and widening the cervical canal has been used by Japanese physicians for more than a century. The reason why it is preferred is that it widens the canal much more slowly and less traumatically than the metal instruments commonly used in the U.S. to widen the canal. If used, it will be removed at this time. If not, the cervix will be dilated (widened) with sterile graduated dilators.

Then, a plastic tube (cannula) attached to a vacuum pump is slowly inserted into the uterus through the cervical canal. The diameter of the cannula depends on the number of weeks of pregnancy. The more pregnant you are, the wider the cannula needs to be.

The cannula is moved back and forth until the tissues of pregnancy are removed. Often after this suction, a curette (a metal instrument with a small loop on the end) is used to check if the suction has removed all the tissue. The entire process takes ten to fifteen minutes.

Immediately afterward, when local anesthetic is used, some women will experience cramping, some faintness, or nausea. Patients are kept under observation until they are feeling well.

A follow-up visit will be arranged at the clinic or with a local physician. If it was necessary to travel some distance for the procedure, an appointment should be made with a clinic or gynecologist when you return home. The appointment is usually scheduled from two to six weeks after the procedure. A 24-hour medical telephone number should be given to you in the event of complication such as fever, heavy bleeding, or pain. You need to keep track of your temperature; anything over 100 degrees Fahrenheit is considered unusual and should be reported to the physician.

It is necessary to avoid intercourse for at least two weeks after the abortion. Don't douche, take a bath, or use tampons for at least that long. You may run a greater risk of infection if you do. Showering is fine; if you don't have a shower, kneel in a shallow tub of water. Although Chinese and Eastern European women are usually given a week's sick leave or more, most women in the United States return to their jobs in one to two days.

The second method of pregnancy termination, also done in the first trimester, is called simply dilation and curettage (D & C). the difference between it and the suction method is that only a curette is used. The operation can be done in a hospital under general anesthetic or on an outpatient basis. The post-pregnancy care is identical. This method has, however, generally been replaced by suction D & C, which is easier, safer, and less time-consuming.

There are complications to watch for after any abortion in the first trimester. Perforation of the uterus as a complication, however, has been overstressed. Simple perforation by a probe or dilator where no suction tube or curette is guided through the perforation will usually repair itself. Infection—inflammation of the lining of the uterus (endometritis) or inflammation of the uterine tubes (salpingitis)—might come from too early intercourse, use of tampons, or douching. Bleeding occurs when the tissues of pregnancy remain on the uterine wall and must be completely removed by additional curettage.

Ectopic pregnancy is not an impossibility. The word ectopic means there is a growing embryo outside the uterus, for example, in the uterine tube. A pregnancy test will be positive and you will not menstruate—just as if the fertilized egg had implanted itself in the uterine wall. Because dilation and curettage only draw out the tissue from the uterus, you will still be pregnant if the fertilized egg is developing outside the uterus. You will no doubt be having pain in the abdominal area if the implantation is in the uterine tube since the uterine tubes are not large enough to maintain the pregnancy. The developing embryo will have to be removed surgically. Women who have become pregnant while wearing an IUD should pay particular attention to this possibility since the IUD prevents, in most cases, the fertilized egg from implanting in the uterine wall, yet it does not prevent the fertilized egg from attaching itself elsewhere.

Pregnancy termination can be done very early in the first trimester—after a missed period and before a pregnancy test can accurately tell you if you are pregnant. (Pregnancy tests are not reliable prior to the sixth week from your last menstrual period. This procedure is done from four to six weeks after the last menstrual period.

It is called early suction dilation and curettage. Early uterine evacuation, mini suction, menstrual extraction, and menstrual regulation are other terms that have been used to describe it. It is almost identical to suction D & C.

The differences, though, are that no anesthetic is required, although it can be given; no dilation of the cervix is necessary since the tissues of pregnancy are minimal and a smaller diameter cannula can be used, similar to the size of the inserter that holds the IUD, and the cost is less. A woman will probably feel cramping similar to strong period cramps.

A missed period does not always mean you are pregnant, but it may. And if you have been having unprotected intercourse or have been haphazardly using contraceptives you should place pregnancy at the top of the list in explanation of a late period.

Because a pregnancy cannot be verified immediately after a missed period, most doctors will encourage a woman to wait for another week or two for confirmation. However, there are cases when there is no doubt in a woman's mind that she is pregnant, especially when she knows her body and is aware of the difference between premenstrual symptoms and symptoms of pregnancy.

A word of caution—there have been cases where women have had this procedure done and have thought of it as "bringing on a late period." Subsequently, when the doctor found early tissues of pregnancy, there was a charge for abortion and the women were not psychologically prepared for this. It is important for any woman to be honest with herself.

There are two possible complications from this early suction D & C. Incomplete evacuation of uterine contents can allow continuation of a pregnancy and you should go back to the clinic if your next menstrual period is delayed. Be watchful for infection. Although this is uncommon, any temperature over 100 degrees Fahrenheit or 38 degrees Centigrade, particularly when associated with lower abdominal pain or tenderness, is reason enough to contact the physician who performed the procedure immediately.

Also, a period similar to your regular period will follow this early suction D & C and if it is unusually long or heavy in flow, contact the physician or clinic.

The second trimester of pregnancy extends from the twelfth to the twenty-fourth week of pregnancy. A woman must be hospitalized for an abortion in the second trimester and with hospitalization, the cost and time involved are greater and the psychological impact is more intense. But familiarity with the procedure can help you cope with the situation by easing anxiety about what is going to happen. Saline solution, the most commonly used fluid for the termination of pregnancies in the second trimester, is injected into the fluid-filled amniotic sac which surrounds the fetus. It disrupts the pregnancy and labor follows. Other fluids containing prostaglandin or urea are used in the same way.

If pregnancy is more than twelve weeks, it is necessary to wait until the sixteenth week of pregnancy before injections of saline or prostaglandin can be safely done. Before the sixteenth week the sac is not filled with enough fluid and there is a danger of injecting concentrated salt solution into the blood stream, which results in serious complications.

Since the risks with this procedure are greater than for a first-trimester pregnancy termination, more lab work is required before the operation. An extensive medical history is taken as well as tests for anemia, Rh negative blood, and a general examination. If saline solution or urea is to be used, local anesthetic is injected over the site on the abdomen where the needle will be inserted. Fluid from the amniotic sac is withdrawn (about 200 milliliters) and replaced with the same amount of saline solution. The injection takes ten to fifteen minutes and one injection is enough to cause abortion in 97% of women. In one to two hours the fetus and placental tissue are destroyed and labor will follow within forty-eight hours. Sometimes other chemicals, like oxytocin (a hormone which causes the uterus to contract) will be given intravenously to shorten the time.

If prostaglandin is used instead of saline solution, the relatively small amount needed to begin labor does not warrant withdrawal of fluid from the amniotic sac. The average time for pregnancy termination with this fluid is around twenty hours.

With a second-trimester pregnancy termination, a woman usually can go home one to two hours after the expulsion of the fetus and afterbirth where there is no unusual bleeding or pain. Some physicians prefer to do a curettage after the fetus and placenta are expelled; some don't. Complications can be lessened by curettage after expulsion of the fetus and placenta. The most common complication is tissue retained in the uterus, which causes bleeding about forty-eight hours after the placenta has been expelled. If this occurs, dilation and curettage of the uterus are necessary.

Concentrated salt solution accidently injected outside the amniotic sac and into the bloodstream is the most serious possible complication of this procedure and can result in

death. Inadvertent injection into the bloodstream of prosto-
glandin results in nausea, diarrhea, and abdominal pain. Urea,
like prostaglandin, in place of concentrated salt solution has a
distinct advantage over saline solution in that it does not lead
to serious complications if accidently injected into the bloodstream. Rupture or laceration of the cervix is more common
when a miscarriage is induced and the cervix is not adequately
dilated. Interruption of normal bood clotting is seen two hours
after pregnancy tissues have been expelled, using the saline
solution method, and usually corrects itself in about six hours.
However, if it does not, other measures such as transfusion
need to be used.

4

WOMEN'S HEALTH CARE

It has been said that civilization can be measured by the amount of soap used. Welcome to civilization.

Manufacturers of soaps, deodorants, and cleaning products rely on our guilt about being dirty to sell their products, and they rely on advertising agencies to create the guilt, for that's their business: manipulating the consumer. Ring around the collar? You *should* feel awful. B.O.? Even God won't like you. Feet stink? Quick, grab your can of Sensual Sole Spray and improve your love life. Bad breath? Well, if you haven't got the media message that you'll lose your job, friends, spouse, then you probably don't have a TV set and are perfectly happy.

The newest deodorant products are the genital deodorants, advertised delicately as "feminine sprays." If you ask a woman what she used fifteen years ago to eliminate "feminine odor" she usually says that she bathed or showered daily. But we've been fed the notion, Madison Avenue style, that we're dirty and we have to keep scrubbing, douching, and spraying in a constant vigil not to offend. Manufacturers have created a demand for a product of questionable value. Germaine Greer pointed out she has yet to see a man overcome by vaginal fumes. The way things are going, men will soon find themselves guilty about "masculine odor." The ad would read: "Is your crotch odor reminiscent of your tennis shoes after a match? Would your woman friend rather hold your gym gear than you? Then use—Foul Ball." Love it.

The alternative to all of these products is ordinary cleanliness. You don't need lots of soap, and scrubbing isn't necessary. The vagina is not dirty and it is not sterile. The same germs are in your mouth as in your vagina. And, as with your mouth, don't put soap or sprays into the vagina! In fact, don't put anything into your vagina you would not put into your mouth.

Perfumed, oily, and flavored preparations, including scented pads and tampons, can be harmful to the vulva and vagina. Many women, because of various advertising campaigns, have suffered from chemical irritation and from burns on the genitals that result in extreme soreness and look as if the genital area had been scalded. If this happens to you, Desitin Ointment applied to the external genitals can keep you comfortable, but only time will heal damaged tissue.

If you feel a need to douche at the end of your period, use one tablespoon of vinegar in a quart of warm water. The solution is cheap, effective, and it is similar to the natural pH of the vagina. If you are douching due to a discharge and it doesn't go away after one or two douches, do get help. Strawberry-flavored or other douches will not cure you, may disguise the problem, and can upset the pH of the vagina.

Itching, burning, a foul discharge with a green tint, sores (whether painful or not), or any area that does not heal should alert you to a problem that needs medical attention.

Yeast infections can happen in women who have never had intercourse. Yeast is part of the natural flora of the vagina—it is always present. But certain situations can cause a rapid population growth of the yeast organism and result in a discharge that is white and curdy (like cottage cheese) in appearance, that causes a burning after intercourse, and won't go away with douching. Situations like stress, increase in warmth due to nylon underwear or pantyhose that hold moisture, or a diet high in carbohydrates (including alcohol) can all cause yeast infections. Practitioners see lots of yeast infections during the holidays and warm weather.

Yeast infections can be easily treated with vaginal suppositories or cream (nystatin is the class name for the medication). If you are taking penicillin or other antibiotics, you should ask your doctor about the possibility of your getting a yeast infection. Antibiotics upset the natural environment of the vagina and may result in an overgrowth of yeast.

The geography of the female genitals is such that the anus, vagina, and urethra are within about two inches of one another. For this reason, microorganisms that are found in one area are often the cause of irritation or infection in another. The urethra, for example, often goes unnoticed until there is an infection in it, at which time itching and burning can occur.

Many times these infections are very simple to treat *if* a woman does not wait too long to get medical help. One way to avoid some infections is to urinate both before and after intercourse. As male and female genitals rub together, the urethra can become clogged with bacteria. A stream of urine can rinse away bacteria from this channel that connects the bladder to the urethral opening. In addition, after a bowel movement be sure to wipe toward the back instead of forward over the vaginal and urethral openings. Or, wipe yourself with a wet cloth. Once again, this keeps bacteria from the bowel away from the other openings. If anal intercourse is your preference, save it for the finale. Bits of fecal matter can easily be transferred into the vagina if anal intercourse is soon followed by vaginal intercourse, and this is bad for the vagina. It may cause non-specific vaginitis.

Cystitis can result when bacteria from the intestine, the vagina, or the skin contaminate the urethra. The major symptoms of cystitis are a burning sensation during urination; the need to urinate often and urgently; and, at times, bloody urine. Cystitis often occurs in otherwise healthy young women who recently have become sexually active; hence, it is sometimes called "honeymoon cystitis." It may be caused, in part, by the swelling and irritation of the urethra during intercourse, with resultant bacterial contamination of the bladder. If the infection is not treated with antibiotics, it may progress to involvement of the kidneys. However, it is easy to diagnose and responds well to treatment. Drinking a glass of water and urinating immediately after intercourse may prevent or decrease recurrences. In addition, urinate when you feel the need; make sure you have some kind of lubrication, whether natural or artificial, during intercourse; and if you begin to feel sore, tell your partner. If changing positions during intercourse doesn't help, then stop. Don't wear tight pants which may rub against your clitoris and urethra and result in irritation or infection. If you have cystitis, avoid drinking coffee, tea, and alcohol. Go get help.

Hemorroids are little pieces of rectal tissue with a blood vessel inside—like varicose veins of the rectum and anus. Both men and women are plagued by hemorroids, and they are common in women just prior to and after delivery. Constipation is usually the chief cause. Drinking eight to ten glasses of water a day prevents the hard stools that can lead to constipation. Additionally, responding to the natural urge of a bowel movement instead of dashing off to work or whatever is a good habit to get into. And, if you have hemorroids already, make a point of avoiding constipation, which is a real irritant.

If you notice small amounts of bright red blood that do not persist beyond three or four days, medical attention is not necessary. However, if bleeding is profuse or dark in color, seek medical attention. If splits or fissures in the tissues have developed or if there is chronic irritation or lots of pain, then surgery might be needed. Taking sitz baths, pushing tissues back into the rectum, and using ointments made specifically for hemorroids can make you more comfortable.

PELVIC EXAM

Perhaps one of the most valuable and yet most maligned aspects of female health care is the pelvic exam. If done by a skilled, caring practitioner it does not have to be a painful or negative experience. If it is—complain!

Basically, a pelvic exam is a medical examination of the lower abdomen and genital area. For someone who knows about female health care, looking at the outer genitals, taking tests, and examining your internal organs gives information about your health. You'll need a pelvic exam before oral contraceptives can be prescribed, an IUD can be inserted, or a diaphragm can be fitted because it is important that your pelvic organs be normal and healthy.

If the cervix were easy to reach and not a sexual part, the procedures necessary would not be embarrassing or have the emotional overtones that a pelvic examination has. Many women respond to these negative feelings by avoiding this examination. This can be a very self-destructive alternative, for the Pap smear can save your life. It is a valuable test for cancer.

Many negative feelings come from learning not to touch our sexual parts and being told not to let other people touch us "down there." Other uncomfortable feelings we have are the result of the mystery of the examination, because nobody tells us what's going on.

So if you feel uncomfortable, it's not surprising. Try a woman physician or a women's health-care specialist. Many clinics such as those run by the Planned Parenthood Organization can offer you an alternative and give you an explanation of the procedure.

It will probably take some time to overcome your feelings about a pelvic examination. One thing that helps is to learn what is being done and why, in order to develop a positive attitude toward the procedure. Feel free to shop around. If one practitioner doesn't explain things or is unsympathetic to your problems, try another one. When you find someone who is interested in you and is informative, work *with* that person. Tensing every muscle in your body and dreading every time you have to have an exam will probably continue to make it an unpleasant experience.

You should have a pelvic exam at least once a year whether you are sexually active or not. With this exam your blood pressure is usually taken, since blood pressure is a valuable indicator of general health. The number of additional tests will vary depending on whether you go to a clinic or a private physician as part of a yearly check-up. Before the exam you will be asked to empty your bladder. A full bladder not only makes you uncomfortable but makes the uterus more difficult for the examiner to feel.

You lie on your back with knees bent and feet supported in metal stirrups. Because your cervix is at the inner end of the vagina, a tool is needed to push apart the walls of the vagina to make the cervix visible. This tool is known as a speculum. It is made of metal or plastic and should be warmed and lubricated with warm water (especially if it is metal) before it is placed in the vagina. You will feel some gentle pressure when the walls of the vagina are pushed apart but this is a normal feeling. The practitioner checks the external genitals first and then looks at the cervix. Ask him or her if you can look at your cervix—it's a neat feeling to see a part of yourself that's so important. The only extra equipment needed is a mirror.

The Pap smear and gonorrhea tests are done with the speculum in place. These tests are painless. The Pap test is a valuable diagnostic tool and can give early warning of cervical or uterine cancer. It is a laboratory test of a sample of cells taken from the cervix and the upper vagina during a pelvic examination. It involves removing surface cells by a gentle rub with a small wooden spatula. These cells are then placed on a glass slide that is sent to a lab. Pap smears are rated on a scale from "perfectly normal smear" to "positive for cancer," with many gradations in between.

The bug that causes gonorrhea grows well in the environment of the cervical canal. Therefore, it is important to get a sample of mucus from this area. A Q-tip with a long handle is used for this purpose, the cotton end being placed in the cervical canal and swirled. The mucus is spread onto a gel-like substance and allowed to stand at a certain temperature. If you have gonorrhea, the bug will grow on the gel.

After these tests are finished, the speculum is removed. Next, it is necessary to check the internal organs such as the uterus and ovaries to see if they are normal. To do this, the practitioner inserts one or two gloved, lubricated fingers into the vagina and will place the other hand on your lower abdomen. This is called a bimanual. The practitioner should also do a recto-vaginal exam, inserting one finger into the rectum and one into the vagina, again feeling the pelvic organs between both hands. In this way any masses behind the uterus or ovaries can be detected and, additionally, cancer of the rectum can be picked up.

After the exam is finished is a good time to ask questions. Was there anything unusual? If the person doing the exam didn't explain what he or she was doing, ask now. If you've had any problems, discuss them with the practitioner—this is the time to get your two cents in. Experiences such as painful intercourse, discharge, or intermenstrual bleeding should be brought to his or her attention.

THE BREAST

Many women have no idea what their breasts should feel and look like. If there were a blemish on your face or a rash on your hands you would probably notice it within a day or two. Would you notice a dimpling in the skin of your breast in a day? Do you even look at your breasts?

The breasts lie over the chest muscles and are formed from fat tissue and glands. They develop for the purpose of nourishing offspring. However, in our society the nourishing function of the breast has become far less important than its seductive capacity and, along with other parts of the body whose exposure is taboo, the breast remains more or less covered. During and after puberty this cover-up becomes more and more important and, while honoring society's demands, a woman also hides her naked breasts from herself. It is ironic that so much attention is given to the breast in our society, yet it remains the leading cause of death, by cancer, in women. Manufacturers will not hesitate to advertise how we can lift, separate, or enlarge our breasts, but rarely do we see much time devoted to taking care of them.

It is estimated that nearly 7 percent of the female population in the United States will develop breast cancer and many women will needlessly die.

The woman who runs the greatest risk of developing breast cancer has one or more of the following characteristics. She has never had children or had her first child after age thirty. She has a history of noncancerous breast disease, particularly in both breasts; she is the daughter of parents with a family history of cancer; her blood relatives (mother, aunts, sisters) have a history of breast cancer; or she did not go through menopause until late in life.

If you don't fit into any of those groups, that doesn't mean you should stop checking your breasts. It means you are less likely to develop cancer of the breast.

When a woman examines her own breasts every month she will be far more sensitive to the formation of a lump than a physician or a women's health-care specialist who is not familiar with her breasts.

Early detection of breast cancer before it has had time to spread to other parts of the body increases a woman's chances for long-term survival and cure.

The best time to examine your breasts is about a week after your menstrual period. At this time there is less hormone stimulation and, as a result, your breasts are less full and tender. This fullness is due to the increase in size of the glands within the breasts. These glands radiate from the nipple as spokes of a wheel radiate from the hub. When a woman gives birth to a baby these glands fill with milk, which is then released through many ducts or channels in the nipple when the baby suckles. There is not just one hole through which the milk flows.

These glands also change at different times in your menstrual cycle. Sometimes the channel of one of these glands becomes blocked and the gland will swell. This is important to know because only one out of every five lumps is cancerous and this is an example of one that isn't.

To examine your breasts, stand in front of the mirror and look at them. Check for any changes in size, shape, position, or color. Look for dimpling, puckering, or an appearance similar to the skin of an orange in or around the nipples. If you notice anything unusual make an appointment at a clinic or with a physician. Most changes or lumps are not cancerous, but you will need to have anything unusual checked to be sure. Now, slowly raise your arms above your head and slowly lower them. Do both breasts lift evenly and fall evenly? This is normal. Both breasts should move freely.

To check underneath your arms, rest your arm on something in order to relax the muscles in your armpit. With the other hand, feel for lumps in your armpit. Then repeat with your other arm.

Lie down on your back and place a folded towel or pillow underneath your right shoulder and put your right arm underneath or behind your head. This will distribute the breast tissue evenly. Press gently, using your left hand, with fingers flat, and make small circular motions around the outside of your breast. You will notice a ridge of firm tissue at the bottom edge of each breast; this is normal. Now repeat what you have just done, but this time one inch closer to the nipple. You will end up making about three or four circles. Feel for any thickening, lump, or hard knot. Then place the folded towel or pillow under your left shoulder and repeat the procedure. Allow yourself enough time to cover every inch of your breasts. Next, gently squeeze the nipple of each breast between your thumb and forefinger. If there is any liquid, whether bloody or not, see your doctor or clinic immediately.

You might find that examining your breasts while taking a shower or bath is easiest because your fingers can glide in the circular motions more easily. But, if your breasts are large, it's best to use the other method. If you find a lump, notice a discharge or any change in your breasts, make an appointment with a clinic or physician immediately, and don't panic.

Remember, only one out of every five lumps is cancerous.

If there is any doubt in the physician's mind, he or she will probably arrange for you to get a breast x-ray called a mammogram.

If you do have a cancerous lump you will know that through your monthly breast self-exam you did everything you possibly could to protect yourself.

RAPE

Even if you do not want to report a sexual assault to the police, you owe it to yourself to establish not only that you are physically all right but to establish the validity of your claim. With the legal system as it stands, the burden of proof is on you. Although your natural instinct is to wash yourself because you feel dirty, you would also be washing away evidence. Do not bathe or douche if there is the slightest possibility that you might want to report. And, get to a medical facility immediately.

The rapist might have given you a sexually transmitted disease (STD). Gonorrhea cultures should be taken from your throat, vagina, and/or anus if the rapist's penis made contact in any of these areas. Blood should be drawn for a syphilis test (VDRL). This test will determine only whether or not you had syphilis at the time of the rape; you will need to be retested in eight weeks to determine if you were infected by the rapist. You also need to return for a gonorrhea check in four to seven days. Tests are not always accurate, so it's safest to repeat the test. The most accurate test is done during a menstrual period.

Remember that until you receive negative results on both your gonorrhea and syphilis tests, you could be spreading an STD.

If intercourse took place between ten and eighteen days

before an expected menstrual period and you are not using the pill or an IUD, you may want to take the morning-after treatment (MAT). This drug is extremely effective in preventing pregnancy; the dosage usually consists of two pills a day for five days, and you must start within seventy-two hours after rape. If you feel ill, check with the doctor rather than stop taking the pills. Pregnancy from a rape can be a very depressing condition, and the discomfort from the pills usually diminishes each day they are taken. Some experts believe that MAT is risky, so you may prefer to wait and have a menstrual extraction or an abortion if necessary. Ask your doctor about the risks before you decide.

The doctor should check for tears around and on the walls of the vagina. You are likely to be both tense and sore and you may need to remind the doctor of those two factors before the examination is begun. If it hurts, don't be afraid to tell the physician.

The doctor should be told of any possible areas of injury— where the rapist hit, squeezed, or pushed you. These areas should be examined.

If you are going to report to the police, complete medical records are important; the results of tests for STD, along with notations of bruises, handprints, and other injuries are potential evidence. If you see a doctor immediately, bruises may not be evident, so you may need a return trip in a couple days. Even if your injuries are not serious, a doctor's notation of them on medical records may be valuable evidence.

Semen should be examined, if it can be found on your body or clothing. Sperm samples should be taken and examined under a microscope, and a record made of the time they were taken.

If you have torn clothing as a result of the rape, show the

doctor, who may be willing to put it in the record. If you possibly can, check your chart before you leave to be sure all possible evidence has been recorded.

Men and boys can also be victims of sexual assault, and the impact on them can be just as traumatic. Although they don't have to worry about pregnancy, they should seek a medical examination immediately (before washing) and save any stained or torn clothing. Tests for STDs should be done right away and in a follow-up visit.

5

SEXUALLY TRANSMITTED DISEASES

For a few years following World War II, it looked as though the venereal diseases were disappearing in the Western world. But it didn't happen. The introduction of oral contraceptives and then of the intrauterine contraceptive devices in the early 1960s led to profound changes in sexual behavior. This sexual liberation mainly involved women as the double standard of sexual behavior began to disappear. As a result, gonorrhea is skyrocketing—increasing at a rate of 15 percent per year since 1963—and a host of other sexually transmitted diseases (STDs) has emerged. Sexually transmitted diseases have reached epidemic proportions.

Among the top twenty STDs only five are traditionally called venereal diseases: gonorrhea, syphilis, chancroid, lymphogranuloma venereum (LGV), and granuloma inguinale. Of these five, only gonorrhea and syphilis are still common in developed countries, while chancroid, LGV, and granuloma inguinale remain common only in underdeveloped countries. Granuloma inguinale causes disfiguring sores on the genitals and pictures of this disease were used during World Wall II in a futile effort to convince troops that sex was not worth the risk. Fortunately, unless you have sex in Port Moresby, New Guinea, or in India, your chances of getting granuloma inguinale are almost zero.

The purpose here is not to prevent sex, but rather to give you a realistic picture of what sexually transmitted disease is today, what you can do to prevent it, and what you should do if you get one. Subsequent sections on treating STD include descriptions of the four most common symptoms or signs, and advice on getting the best treatment. (After reading these sections, you will not have to go to the library to check out a book on VD "for a sick friend" if you develop symptoms.)

There has been an explosion of new information on STD in the past five years, the result of a multimillion dollar international research program, but this information has scarcely begun to reach the public. All the popular books about VD have been historical or have focused on gonorrhea and syphilis while mostly ignoring the other important sexually transmitted diseases. Most information presented to students in the classroom or to the public via the mass media is either irrelevant or misleading. To complicate matters, much of the new information has not even filtered down to the level of a family physician.

For example, most doctors have never heard of the two bacteria that cause nongonococcal urethritis—the most common sexually transmitted disease in men. When you go to the doctor for a VD "check up," chances are you will get tested for only one of the common STDs—gonorrhea. A man without symptoms may not get tested at all.

Did you know that the type of STD you get may be determined by the type of contraceptive you use? Do you know why gonorrhea is more serious than a simple cold below the belt? Did you realize that most men walking around with gonorrhea right now do not have any symptoms of it? Do you know which of the common venereal diseases today are the worst—more serious than either gonorrhea or syphilis? What do you know about the sexually transmitted disease that keeps coming back to haunt you—genital herpes?

Did you ever ask yourself, before having sex with a new partner: "What are the chances I might get VD, and what could I do to prevent it?" If you are married, did you ever wonder after having sex with a pickup or casual acquaintance, how long you would have to wait to be sure you did not develop signs of STD so it would be safe to have sex again with your spouse? If you did get one of the common forms of STD, would you know how to recognize it before you passed it on? Do you know the best place to go for treatment? Read on, to discover the answers to these and many other intriguing questions.

The sexually transmitted diseases include the original five venereal diseases and a growing number of others which are now known to be or are suspected of being transmitted by some form of sexual intercourse. The number one STD is, without doubt, unwanted pregnancy. If you skipped the discussion of contraception, go back and read about that first. The remaining ten top sexually transmitted diseases of the 1970s and the ten runners up are listed below in approximate order of importance:

Top Ten Sexually
Transmitted Diseases

1) Gonorrhea
2) Genital herpes
3) Cytomegalovirus infection
4) Chlamydia infection
5) T-mycoplasma infection

6) Hepatitis B
7) Syphilis
8) Pubic lice
9) Genital warts
10) Trichomonas vaginitis

Ten Leading Contenders

11) Nonspecific vaginitis   16) Granuloma inguinale
12) Yeast infection   17) Chancroid
13) Infectious mononucleosis   18) Shigella dysentery
14) Scabies   19) Amebic dysentery
15) Genital molluscum contagiosum 20) Giardiasis

Most of these twenty infections probably sound unfamiliar. Some are often spread nonsexually as well as sexually, but many of them have become epidemic among sexually active people, and the story of how they are spread, of the diseases they cause, and of the modern attempts to control them is a fascinating one.

Despite all the efforts of sociologists and venereologists, no one yet fully understands why STD is booming. The number one reason may be sexual liberation which followed development of newer methods of contraception. A second reason is that the introduction of oral contraceptives and of the IUD cut down on the use of other contraceptive methods, such as the condom and vaginal spermicides, which had offered some protection against STD.

A third reason is that women using oral contraceptives may actually become more susceptible to certain STDs. This is still very speculative and controversial among experts, but it may not be a coincidence that each of the top four STDs are caused by microbes which live in an area of the body which is greatly influenced by oral contraceptives. In women, a natural home for gonorrhea, genital herpes, cytomegalovirus, and chlamydia is the tiny part of the cervix where the flattened cells which cover the visible part of the cervix join with the mucous membrane lining of the inner cervix. This area is normally covered by a mucous plug, but during pregnancy, or after about six months of oral contraceptive use, this "junctional zone" moves out into a more exposed position on the visible part of the cervix. This exposed zone is called ectropion. It is possible that by producing ectropion, oral contraceptives make the cervix more susceptible to these microbes, or more likely to transmit them.

Whatever the reason for the STD epidemic, the sexually active person—now more than ever—needs to have a realistic understanding of STD. Unfortunately, many of us first learned about STD from educators who dealt in fear instead of facts. However alarming the following description of STDs may seem, keep in mind that the odds are against your getting one of them if you and your friends conform to the average national standards of sexual behavior. Even if you do catch STD, the rest of this book will tell you how easy it is to get rid of most of them. The last thing we want to do is cause an epidemic of frightened teenagers who run to the VD clinics for checkups after their first intercourse. Knowledge about STD should not keep anyone from having a healthy sex life.

We will concentrate on those treatable STDs like gonorrhea, which cause problems only if they are neglected and which are important for you to be able to recognize before complications develop; and on the still untreatable ones like genital herpes, hepatitis B, and cytomegalovirus infection, which are important for you to try to avoid. We will not discuss diseases like lymphogranuloma venereum or granuloma inguinale, which are too rare for you to worry about.

GONORRHEA

About three million cases of gonorrhea, informally called "clap," occurred in the United States in 1975. From 5 to 8 percent of the people in the United States between the ages of twenty and twenty-four caught it last year. This is many times higher than the rate of gonorrhea in most other Western countries. The number of cases of gonorrhea occurring per year has begun to fall in Scandinavian countries, but not in the United States.

The reasons for the much higher rates of gonorrhea in the U.S. are complex, but the biggest reason is probably that in this country the infected person (or the person's doctor) is less likely to inform all sex partners who have been exposed. This is very inconsiderate. Gonorrhea is easily treated and cured, but it can be very bad for you if it is not treated.

Another big reason gonorrhea is more common than it needs to be in all countries is that so many people have misconceptions about the disease. For example, it is still taught that all men with gonorrhea have symptoms but that women do not develop symptoms. This and other half-truths serve to confuse rather than clarify understanding of the disease.

Here are the essential facts you need to know about gonorrhea. It is caused by a bacteria, the gonococcus, which commonly infects the urethra, the cervix, the anus, and the throat. In women, all four sites may be infected, but the cervix is almost always involved and is the most important site of infection, since spread from the cervix to the uterine tubes causes the most serious complication of gonorrhea.

In homosexual men, infection of the urethra, anal canal, and throat are all common, but in heterosexual men, infection usually involves only the urethra. Fellatio (oral sex with the penis) is three or four times as likely to result in gonorrhea of the throat as cunnilingus (which usually involves oral sex with the clitoris). Therefore, homosexual men and heterosexual women are more likely than heterosexual men or homosexual women to acquire throat infections.

Gonorrhea sometimes causes infection of the throat only, without a simultaneous genital or anal infection. Gonococcal throat infection may cause a sore throat, and, like infection of the other sites, can lead to blood stream infection, but it is probably not very contagious to other people. It is very unlikely that one could get it by kissing (even with tongues).

In men, gonorrhea usually causes burning at the tip of the penis when urine is passed, and a discharge of pus from the opening of the urethra. Although other infections can cause the same symptoms, they are practically always sexually transmitted too. If you ever had such symptoms but just waited until they subsided instead of getting them treated, there is an excellent chance you became a carrier of gonorrhea or some other STD.

Gonorrhea causes symptoms in women as well as in men. Do not wait and see if the symptoms go away, because they will. But the gonorrhea will remain, perhaps for as long as six months to a year, during which time the gonorrhea could flare up and cause serious complications, could be given to a new sex partner, or could be transmitted during childbirth to a newborn infant. It is very important for any sexually active person to be able to recognize the symptoms of gonorrhea when they occur.

When a man with symptoms of burning during urination or discharge from the penis goes to see a doctor, the doctor always considers the possible diagnosis of gonorrhea. However, when a woman develops symptoms of gonorrhea, much of the time—maybe most of the time—the doctor does not think of gonorrhea. This is partly because several other conditions which are not sexually transmitted can cause identical symptoms, and partly because some doctors do not feel comfortable asking women about their sexual encounters. Therefore, it is especially important for a woman to know what symptoms she is likely to develop if she catches gonorrhea, and to make sure she is tested for gonorrhea when she gets examined.

In women, gonorrhea commonly causes one or more of the

following symptoms: increased discharge from the vagina (caused by infection of the cervix); abnormal menstrual bleeding (infection of the uterus); pain in the low abdomen (infection of the uterus and tubes); or burning on urination (infection of the urethra).

Women who develop these symptoms should always be checked for gonorrhea. In a study in Memphis, one-third of women who had burning when they urinated or had unexplained menstrual bleeding had gonorrhea. In spite of this evidence, there are undoubtedly thousands of women every year in the U.S. who consult physicians because of these symptoms but are not tested for gonorrhea. Many women with burning on urination receive only a telephone consultation and are simply referred without examination to the nearest pharmacy, where they are given antibiotics for a "bladder infection" or "honeymoon cystitis." These antibiotics usually are not enough to cure gonorrhea if it is the real cause of the symptoms. Pain in the low abdomen is the most dangerous symptom of gonorrhea in women. It could indicate a condition which, if not attended to immediately, could lead to sterility by damaging the uterine tubes through which the ova must pass.

We do not know exactly what percentage of men or women who get gonorrhea develop symptoms, but we believe most do. One study in which U.S. Navy men in the Western Pacific were repeatedly tested for gonorrhea before and after sexual exposures showed that over 95 percent of men who caught gonorrhea from prostitutes developed the first signs of infection within two to seven days after exposure: a discharge of pus from the opening of the penis and, often, burning with urination. However, there is some evidence that certain strains of gonococcus which can cause infection without symptoms are more common in the U.S. than in the Western Pacific.

Most men who develop symptoms of gonorrhea seek and obtain treatment. However, as with women, some men who develop symptoms ignore them. Others never develop symptoms and become carriers for months. The key point is that most people in the community who have gonorrhea at this moment either have ignored their symptoms or have no symptoms. This is who you usually catch gonorrhea from: someone who has ignored the symptoms or never had them. The same principle applies to all sexually transmitted diseases. Therefore, do not assume that the person you got an STD from will eventually figure out he (or she) has it and will get it taken care of. If you don't tell him (or her), he probably will not get it taken care of until somebody else tells him he is infected.

The two main complications that can follow gonorrhea are pelvic inflammatory disease and blood stream invasion (also known as disseminated gonococcal infection).

Pelvic inflammatory disease (PID) occurs when bacteria spread from the vagina and cervix up through the lining of the uterus and into the uterine tubes, and eventually spill out the open ends of the tubes into the lower pelvic abdominal cavity. At least 15 to 20 percent of women who get gonorrhea develop PID. Early treatment of gonorrhea would reduce that rate. At least five hundred thousand cases of PID occurred in the U.S. in 1975 and about half of them were caused by gonorrhea.

This upward spread of bacteria into the tubes is most likely to happen during menstruation, and the symptoms of PID usually begin during or soon after the menstrual period. Bacteria and viruses can attach themselves to sperm, so it is also possible that microbes can reach the uterine cavity and uterine tubes by riding "piggy back" on sperm.

The risk of developing PID is closely related to the type of contraception a woman uses. Tubal ligation helps prevent PID since bacteria are unable to spread beyond the part of the tube which has been tied. Women who have had hysterectomies are very resistant to gonorrhea and hardly ever develop PID. In contrast, the IUD provides an easy access route for bacteria to climb from the cervix and vagina into the uterine cavity, and women wearing an IUD have a two-and-a-half to nine times increased risk of developing PID. This risk is greatest during the first month after insertion, but the risk of PID remains increased during at least the first three years the IUD is in place, and probably for the entire time the IUD is worn.

A recent Swedish study found that women who had previously been pregnant were much safer with an IUD than women who had never been pregnant. This important finding has not been confirmed elsewhere and should not be taken as gospel yet.

About half of all cases of PID in IUD users would have occurred anyway, but the other half wouldn't have occurred if the woman had not been using the IUD. Although the Dalkon shield has had the most publicity, no type of IUD has been shown to be free of this hazard.

As mentioned earlier, women using oral contraceptives may be more susceptible to catching gonorrhea than other women. However, once they catch gonorrhea, the oral contraceptive actually seems to protect them from developing PID by preventing spread of the infection from the cervix up into the tubes. There are several possible explanations for this. One idea is that the cervical mucus becomes thicker in women taking oral contraceptives, and this might prevent bacteria-carrying sperm from wiggling through the cervix and into the uterine cavity.

Many women who have had PID will develop further complications of PID in the future. One complication is repeated attacks of PID which will develop in about one-third of women within a year after treatment of the first episode of PID. These repeated attacks probably occur because the first attack of PID damaged the tubes and made them susceptible to infection by bacteria which are normally present in the vagina and periodically wash up into the tube during menstruation, but wouldn't ordinarily cause infection in an undamaged tube. A second major complication is infertility as a result of scarring and obstruction of the tubes, which prevents passage of the ovum into the uterus. A third complication is tubal pregnancy, also known as ectopic pregnancy, which can happen when an ovum becomes fertilized but becomes hung up in the scarred tube where it eventually implants itself. This must be treated by surgical removal of the tube. Finally, chronic pelvic pain can be caused by bands of scar tissue which form between the uterus and the abdominal wall. This pain is usually worse while standing or walking. The problem can sometimes be treated surgically by a procedure called "lysis of adhesions": cutting the scar tissue and freeing the uterus from the abdominal wall. Scar tissue and pain often come back and, in severe cases, can only be treated by a hysterectomy.

Gonococcal infection spreads into the blood stream more often in women than in men, partly because menstruation makes women more susceptible to blood stream invasion. Once gonococci enter the blood stream, they tend to lodge in two places: the joints, where they cause arthritis (pain, swelling, redness); and the skin of the arms and legs, where they cause somewhere between five and twenty sores to appear— sores which resemble blood blisters, insect bites, or infected hair follicles. The heart valves and covering of the brain can also become infected but this is rare.

The spread of the disease in this fashion is called dissemination gonococcal infection (DGI). The only strains of gonococcus which can cause DGI are those which are not killed as soon as they enter the blood stream. In the United States, these strains are most heavily concentrated in the Northwest. In Seattle, about half of all new cases of arthritis in hospitalized young adults are caused by gonorrhea, but arthritis due to gonorrhea is less common in some other parts of the U.S.

GENITAL HERPES

Genital herpes is the disease which keeps many venereal disease specialists monogamous. It is increasingly more common, and we suspect that among the well educated—the readers of this book, for example—genital herpes may be just about as common as gonorrhea. It has a nasty habit of recurring, even without sexual contact, and there is currently no known cure for it. It is caused by a virus called Herpes simplex virus, also known as Herpesvirus hominis, or HVH for short. HVH is closely related to other viruses which appear to be spread by sexual intercourse (cytomegalovirus) or by kissing (herpes EB virus, the cause of infectious mononucleosis).

Only ten years ago, it was discovered there were actually two types of Herpesvirus hominis, called type one and type two. Type one HVH causes fever blisters (cold sores) of the mouth, while type two HVH causes genital herpes. Once in a while, as a result of oral sex, someone gets a sore throat or fever blisters of the mouth caused by type two HVH, or genital herpes caused by type one HVH. But overall, type one HVH causes 95 percent of infections above the waist, and type two HVH causes 95 percent of infections below the waist. Probably about one-third of the readers of this book have already had type one HVH infection, and a smaller but growing proportion will eventually get type two infection.

The first infection with type one HVH is usually in childhood and is transmitted, like many childhood diseases, from another infected child or adult by kissing, sharing eating utensils or toilet articles, and so on. It causes severe sore throat, ulcers in the mouth, and fever. The virus then travels up the nerves which run from the mouth toward the brain and takes up permanent residence in nerve cells at the base of the skull. From these nerve cells, the virus periodically, throughout life, can "reactivate" and travel back down the nerve to cause fever blisters (cold sores) at the edge of the lip. Reactivation seems to be caused by fever, by exposure to sun, by an injury to the lip, or by physical or emotional stress. One prominent genital herpes researcher develops fever blisters every time he is asked to deliver a lecture on herpes virus infection.

Genital herpes infection, on the other hand, is nearly always transmitted by sexual intercourse or oral sex, although rare exceptions have occurred—for example, children with fever blisters on the mouth can accidently spread the virus to the genitals with their fingers. If you are one of the millions of adults who suffer repeatedly from cold sores and you have oral sex with someone when you have a cold sore on your lip, there is a good chance your sex partner will develop genital herpes. Therefore you should definitely not perform oral sex when you have cold sores present. Since your fever blister probably was caused by type one HVH, your sex partner's genital infection will also be due to type one HVH. Should you also avoid giving oral sex even between bouts of cold sores? If you are subject to repeated attacks of cold sores, then type one HVH is present in your saliva about one day out of every fifty, on the average, in between the bouts. There is a chance, then, that you could spread the virus by oral sex even when you don't have fever blisters, but the chance is very small.

One controversial study in Boston showed that half of all genital herpes infections were due to type one virus, and this led to speculation that the current epidemic of genital herpes was caused by an increase in oral sex. However, all other recent studies continue to show that about 95 percent of all genital herpes infection are still caused by type two HVH and that these type two infections are nearly all acquired by sexual intercourse.

Your system has a defense against invading foreign bodies such as bacteria and viruses. For example, when a herpes virus enters the bloodstream, the white blood cells attack the virus directly in hand-to-hand combat and also form antibodies which act like bullets to kill the virus. These antibodies last for years after the initial infection, and although they do not completely prevent recurrent herpes, they do persist in your blood where they can be detected as evidence of previous herpes infection. Blood antibodies to type two HVH can be found in nearly 80 percent of prostitutes, 20 to 60 percent of adults of low socioeconomic status, 10 percent of adults of high socioeconomic status, and only 3 percent of celibate women. This indicates that genital herpes is an extremely common infection among sexually active adults.

The earliest symptom of genital herpes is a small red bump (papule) which generally appears two to eight days after sex with an infected person. There are usually several of these papules located on the penis or labia. The papules develop rapidly into tiny painful blisters filled with clear fluid and containing millions of highly infectious virus particles. As white blood cells move into the blisters to combat the virus, the fluid becomes cloudy, and the blister is now called a pustule. The pustule then ruptures, leaving a small painful wet open sore which continues to shed infectious virus. New blisters continue to form for about ten days.

After about ten days from the first appearance of the bump, crusts form over the sore, infectiousness and pain gradually subside, and healing follows. Occasionally, sores hang on for thirty days or more before healing occurs. During the first ten days, many infected persons experience fever, burning on urination (caused by virus growing in the urethral canal), or a painful swelling of lymph glands in the groin.

During the first genital infection, nearly all women have sores on the cervix in addition to those on the labia. These cervical ulcers are painless but they do cause a noticeable vaginal discharge. Herpes virus may last in the cervix for up to ten days after all sores on the labia have healed. Women probably remain infectious until the virus disappears from the cervix, so to be safe they should avoid intercourse until about ten days after the sores on the labia have healed. Once in a while, genital herpes lesions may be so trivial that they go unnoticed, and the individual doesn't know he has genital herpes until he gives it to a sex partner. Some women have genital herpes involving only the cervix, without any ulcers on the labia, and thus may never know they have had the infection.

In a few cases the virus spreads via the blood stream to the covering of the brain (viral meningitis). This causes a severe headache and a stiff neck for several days, but it is nearly always followed by a complete recovery.

The majority of people who catch genital herpes infection have one or more repeated episodes after the first episode has healed. During the first episode, type two HVH travels up nerves from the infected genital area until the virus reaches the nerve cells which lie next to the lower part of the spinal cord. The virus remains in an inactive state in these nerve cells without damaging the cells for the rest of the lifetime of the individual. Periodically thereafter, however, reactivation of the dormant virus within these nerve cells causes the virus to retrace its path back down the nerve to the genitals. This reactivation of dormant virus is called a relapse. It is important to understand that these relapses can occur as long as several

years after the first episode. For example, a man may catch
genital herpes from his wife and accuse her of having just
caught a sexually transmitted disease. But she may have
actually caught the infection years earlier and passed it on to
her husband during a relapse.

Once you have caught genital herpes infection, do you become immune to catching it again from someone else (even
though you are susceptible to developing relapses of your own
infection)? In other words, if you had sex with someone who
had open genital herpes sores, would you catch it again and
come down with it two to seven days later? The answer to this
is not known, but humans who have recovered from herpes
infection can be reinfected by experimentally inoculating
them again with the same virus. It is therefore possible that
you could catch herpes again from someone else, but even so,
most repeated episodes of genital herpes after the first attack
probably represent reactivation of your own dormant infection (relapses).

People who have repeated bouts of type one HVH fever
blisters may wonder if they are also more likely than the average person to have severe attacks of genital herpes if they
catch type two genital infection. The answer isn't definitely
known, but it seems they may actually be somewhat more resistant to type two HVH infection than the average person,
perhaps because the antibodies they have built up to type one
virus protect them against the closely related type two virus.
Nonetheless, people who have had fever blisters can definitely still catch type two HVH genital infection if they are
exposed.

As we have said, the majority of people who catch genital
herpes infection have one or more relapses. The first relapse
develops an average of six to eight weeks after the initial lesions have completely healed. As with type one infection of the

mouth, the relapses of genital herpes due to type two herpes virus are less severe than the first episode and begin to heal after an average of only four days. Although often painful, they usually are not accompanied by fever, swollen lymph glands, or burning pain during urination.

We don't know why some people have many relapses while others do not. Some women connect relapses to menstruation, and some people believe they are more likely to develop a relapse during the summer months. Men often relapse within a day or two after intercourse. Genital herpes does seem to recur less and less often with the passage of time after the first episode. The potential for relapsing and for spreading the infection to others causes emotional stress and sexual problems in many individuals. People who have had genital herpes are anxious to know whether the fact that they always carry type two HVH means that they are always infectious for other people with whom they may have sex in the future.

For these people, there is good news and bad news. The good news is that when a large group of men and women who have had genital herpes were carefully reexamined at regular intervals in a recent study, type two HVH could rarely be found in their genital area, except when lesions were visible on the penis or labia. This suggests that if an individual is careful to inspect his genitals and does not see any herpes lesions, he will not be infectious.

On the other hand, the bad news is that in other studies of VD clinic patients, type two HVH has been recovered from the urethra of 2 to 3 percent of all men without lesions, and from the cervix of 4 percent of all women without lesions.

Furthermore, when an individual named as the suspected infector of a person with a new genital herpes infection is interviewed, he or she usually does not recall having had any lesions at the time of sexual exposure. It seems possible that herpes, like gonorrhea, is spread by people who have no lesions or small nonpainful lesions which they ignore or never even notice.

The two major potential complications of genital herpes are very serious but, fortunately, are relatively uncommon. They are infection of the newborn and cancer of the cervix.

Most infections of the newborn are acquired during birth, when the mother has active genital HVH infection at the time of delivery, after rupture of the amniotic membranes (bag of water) and during the passage through the birth canal. Since most genital herpes infections are due to type two virus, type two HVH is the cause of most of these infections of the newborn.

It has been estimated that HVH infection of the newborn occurs in as many as one in every thirty-five hundred pregnancies in women in disadvantaged populations and less often in women of middle or upper socioeconomic status. The greatest risk of serious infections of the newborn occurs when the mother is actually experiencing her first infection right at the time of delivery. The risk of serious infection in the infant is less if the mother is having a relapse of genital herpes at the time of delivery. Women who have had genital herpes can be reassured that the risk of transmitting the infection to a future baby is very small, probably less than one in a thousand, if open sores are not present at the time of delivery. Infection of the newborn can involve its skin, mouth, eyes, bloodstream, and/or brain, and can be mild or severe. About half the babies who become infected will be severely damaged or killed by the infection.

If the mother has genital herpes lesions (vesicles, pustules, or ulcers) at the time of delivery, a Caesarean section performed before or within four hours after the rupture of the membranes will probably reduce the risk of infecting the child.

A Caesarean section itself has some risk, and the decision as to whether an infant should be delivered vaginally or by C-section when the mother has genital herpes is never a simple one. Unfortunately, as of 1976, no form of treatment is known to be effective for herpes virus infection of the newborn.

Cancer of the cervix is the second most common form of cancer in women (cancer of the breast is first). The low rates of cancer of the cervix in nuns first suggested the possibility that a sexually transmitted agent caused this form of cancer. A recent study at Johns Hopkins showed that the risk of developing cancer of the cervix was increased among the wives of men who had previously been married to other women with cancer of the cervix. These men may be sexually transmitting an agent responsible for cancer of the cervix. Much evidence suggests that this infectious agent is type two Herpesvirus hominis but, like the early data which linked smoking with cancer of the lung, the evidence is circumstantial.

About 2 percent of women who live into old age will develop cancer of the cervix during their lifetime. It is known that the risk is higher among women who have had genital herpes, but it is not yet known exactly how much higher. In Atlanta, very preliminary results from an ongoing study suggest the risk of developing precancerous changes in the cervix is four or five times higher for women who have had genital herpes than for women who have never had the disease. One Swedish study suggested the risk was highest for those who had first had genital herpes between ages fifteen and nineteen.

Typically, precancerous disease of the cervix first appears in women in their late thirties and eventually leads to invasive cancer in women in their forties, although younger or older women can also be affected. Therefore, it is very important that women who have had genital herpes obtain cervical Pap smears every twelve months for the rest of their lives, since cancer of the cervix or precancerous conditions are almost always curable if detected early. So far, it still is not known whether type one HVH infection of the cervix carries the same risk of cancer of the cervix as type two HVH infection. It also is not yet known whether type two HVH infection is associated with genital cancers in men.

If you've gotten the impression that genital herpes is the worst sexually transmitted disease today, you may be right, but it isn't hopeless. As far as the two most serious complications are concerned, life-threatening infection of the newborn is extremely rare unless the baby is born during the first attack of genital herpes, and cancer of the cervix is preventable by annual Pap smears.

One good thing about catching herpes is that once you've gotten it, you probably have less chance of catching it from someone else again—you just have to worry about giving it to someone else. Because of this we propose the formation of a new organization called Herpes Anonymous—a secret society of sexually active adults who have had genital herpes. You'll be able to recognize fellow members at parties or singles bars because they'll be wearing their buttons, which will look something like this:

CYTOMEGALOVIRUS

We debated whether or not to say anything about this one, but decided to go ahead. Some might object to ranking it among sexually transmitted diseases because the evidence it is transmitted sexually is still inconclusive. In any case, cytomegalovirus (CMV) is a very important virus because it causes birth defects. In fact, with rubella (German measles) coming under control since rubella vaccine was introduced, CMV has become the most important known infectious cause of birth defects.

CMV can be found in the saliva, urine, blood, or genital secretions of infected individuals and it can infect people of all ages. Ten to 15 percent of women carry CMV in their cervix during pregnancy. In the U.S., about 1 percent of babies acquire the infection before they are born, and another 5 percent pick it up at the time of birth as they pass through the infected cervix. Those who get infected in the uterus before birth run the highest risk of birth defects—particularly of mental retardation and hearing defects.

It is believed that the major risk of congenital birth defects caused by CMV occurs when the mother is first exposed to CMV just before conception or during pregnancy. It is also believed that new CMV infections of young women of child-bearing age may well be sexually transmitted. Clearly, this is a big problem, and this is why we consider this infection to be potentially one of the most important sexually transmitted diseases. There is no treatment for it, and no vaccine to prevent it. This doesn't necessarily mean there is nothing that can be done about it. One logical precaution is that women who are pregnant or who are trying to get pregnant could avoid having sex with a new sex partner, in order to avoid catching CMV infection at the critical time when the fetus can be damaged.

The idea that CMV is transmitted sexually is relatively new—in fact CMV is probably the newest of the STDs. Although some people first become infected around the time of birth or later in childhood, it is after the onset of puberty that most new infections occur in the Western world. Soon after puberty, new infections start appearing in sexually active people, but not in celibate women. Further evidence that CMV is spread sexually is provided by the fact that CMV can be found in the cervix of up to 29 percent of women attending VD clinics, but as few as 2 percent of women examined in a gynecology clinic. CMV is also carried by men in the semen where the virus can be seen by special microscopic studies to be attached to spermatozoa; about one out of every ten male university students has CMV in his semen.

These are the facts which indicate that CMV is carried in the genital tract of young adults and may be transmitted sexually. It is easy to imagine how a man who carries CMV in his semen could infect the susceptible cells of the cervix of his sex partner during ejaculation. It is less clear how a woman with CMV infection of the cervix might spread the virus sexually to a man, since CMV does not seem to cause infection of the urethra or penis. It is likely that CMV can also be spread by swapping saliva during kissing.

The disease produced by CMV in the young adult is called CMV mononucleosis and causes fever which lasts for several days or weeks. About 90 percent of infectious mononucleosis cases are caused by a related virus called herpes EB virus. EB virus mononucleosis has been known as "the kissing disease" since it was discovered that West Point cadets developed epidemics of it when they returned from Christmas vacation (being West Point cadets, presumably they engaged in nothing more dishonorable than kissing). The remaining 10 percent of cases of mono are usually caused by CMV. This virus infects not only the cervix and semen, but can also be found in saliva, urine, and blood. CMV infects one special type of white blood cell and lives in these cells for life without causing any symptoms of disease. However, if the body's immunity is lowered later in life, by cancer or cancer treatment or other disease, the CMV can move out of the white cells into other tissues and cause fatal damage to the lungs and other organs.

NONGONOCOCCAL URETHRITIS AND RELATED INFECTIONS CAUSED BY CHLAMYDIA AND T—MYCOPLASMA

Nongonococcal urethritis (NGU) is the most common problem seen in STD clinics. "Urethritis" means inflammation of the urethra, and nongonococcal means not due to gonorrhea.

NGU produces symptoms in men but generally not in women, even though recent evidence shows that women do carry the bacteria which cause NGU. This is just the opposite of trichomonas infection, which causes symptoms in women but generally not in men.

The symptoms of NGU in men are just like those of gonorrhea—a discharge of pus from the urethra, and often mild burning at the tip of the penis during urination. Overall, NGU is twice as common as gonorrhea in the U.S. Among male college students, and probably among most of the men who are wise enough to be reading this book, NGU is actually ten times as common as gonorrhea. Think about that the next time you think you have the clap.

It used to be thought that NGU was caused by too much sex or too little sex, by coffee, alcohol, spicy foods or allergy, or by anxiously "milking" the penis to try to squeeze out a drop of discharge after intercourse, or by straining during heavy exercise. However, the only straining which leads to NGU is that associated with sexual intercourse.

The cause of NGU—actually there are at least two causes—was uncertain up until about 1974. That NGU is infectious rather than caused by allergy or irritants or injury of the urethra is established by the fact that antibiotics make it go away, and antibiotics taken just after intercourse actually prevent it. That this infection is sexually transmitted is shown by the fact that it does not occur in sexually inactive men. On

Navy ships, small waves of new cases of NGU occur after every liberty period in port. The incubation period is longer than that of gonorrhea, usually from one to three weeks after sexual exposure.

One of the causes of NGU is now known to be small bacteria called chlamydia (pronounced klah-mi-dee-ah) which are responsible for 40 to 50 percent of all cases. Chlamydia are known to be sexually transmitted, and can be grown from the cervix of three-quarters of the women named as sex partners by men with NGU caused by chlamydia.

Although women with chlamydia of the cervix often have inflammation of the cervix and a discharge of pus from the vagina, this often goes unnoticed. The infection can then hang on for a long time during which a woman can pass the infection on to other men. If she becomes pregnant while chlamydia are present in the cervix, at delivery they contaminate the eyes of the infant, producing a chronic infection which can lead to mild scarring of the cornea of the eyes. (Chlamydia have now replaced the gonococcus as the most common cause of eye infection in the newborn.)

Chlamydia also produce two other important diseases, trachoma and lymphogranuloma venereum (LGV). Trachoma, an eye infection, is the most important infectious cause of blindness in underdeveloped areas of the world but is uncommon in the U.S. LGV is one of the five classical venereal diseases, but one which is now too uncommon in the U.S. to warrant further discussion here. (If you live in Washington, D.C., you may want to find out more about it; for some reason, one-third of all cases of LGV reported each year in the U.S. are reported from our nation's capital.)

The cause of the remaining 50 to 60 percent of NGU cases —those not caused by chlamydia—is still not certain, but recent evidence implicates bacteria known as T-strain mycoplasma (also called ureaplasma). T-strains are known to be sexually transmitted and may well be the first sexually transmitted bacteria to be acquired by most people. For example, over two-thirds of college women who have had two or more sex partners carry T-strains in the vagina, as do 80 to 90 percent of female STD clinic patients.

Symptoms of NGU will usually go away over a period of two to three months, even without treatment. But the disappearance of the symptoms does not mean the disappearance of the chlamydia or T-strains from the urethra, and there is the risk, if there is no treatment, that infection may spread to the prostate or the epididymis. Another possible complication of NGU is an unusual form of arthritis known as Reiter's syndrome which includes inflammation of the joints, skin, eyes, and the urethra, and which usually lasts several months but is not crippling.

At the present time, if you did not have any symptoms but just wanted to go to a doctor to find out if you were carrying chlamydia or T-strains, you probably could not do so since most physicians' laboratories are not set up to test for either of these bacteria.

NOT FOR HOMOSEXUAL MEN ONLY: SERUM HEPATITIS AND SYPHILIS

Serum hepatitis (or hepatitis B) and syphilis are probably the two most serious STDs for homosexual men. Although these diseases are by no means limited to gay men, the chances of getting serum hepatitis or syphilis are at least ten times greater for a homosexual man than for a heterosexual man or a woman. Both diseases can have serious complications.

Hepatitis (inflammation of the liver) causes blood pigments which are normally destroyed by the liver to accumulate in the blood, turning the skin and eyes yellow. Hepatitis can be caused by allergic reactions to drugs, toxic substances which damage the liver, or by certain virus infections. The two most common causes of viral hepatitis have only recently been discovered and are called hepatitis A virus and hepatitis B virus. Both types can be so mild as to go undetected, but hepatitis B virus—the type which has been found to be common in homosexual men—causes the more severe form of hepatitis. About 90 percent of the people who are sick enough with type B hepatitis to see a doctor recover within a few weeks; 1 percent die during the acute illness (most of those who die are elderly), about 3 percent develop a progressive form of hepatitis which is sometimes fatal; and 6 percent develop a persistent form of hepatitis which takes months to heal. Perhaps one in ten adults who acquire hepatitis B virus infection becomes a long-term carrier of hepatitis B virus.

The blood serum of all carriers contains the outer shell of hepatitis B viruses. The shells circulating in the blood stream of some carriers are empty, while in other carriers (the exact percentage is not yet known), the shells actually enclose infectious virus particles. These carriers are often completely normal with no evidence of hepatitis, but if their blood is used for a blood transfusion, it can cause hepatitis in the person who receives the transfusion. For this reason, type B hepatitis has been known as serum hepatitis.

For a long time it was thought that serum hepatitis only occurred in people who received blood transfusions or in drug addicts who used needles which became contaminated with another addict's blood. It was known that young men living in larger cities had an unusually high rate of type B hepatitis, but it was not until 1973 and 1974 that four separate reports from London called attention to the fact that most men with hepatitis B virus infection who were not addicts or had not had a transfusion were homosexual. There are two main types of hepatitis B virus, known as "ay" and "ad." So far it looks like about 90 percent of infections in addicts are caused by type "ay," while 90 percent of infections in homosexual men are caused by type "ad." Maybe this means that there is a sub-culture of addicts who spread one type of virus, while the homosexual subculture spreads another. Approximately 5 per-cent of homosexual men examined in VD clinics or steam baths, and only .5 percent or less of heterosexual VD clinic patients, are carriers of hepatitis B virus. The percentage of homosexual men who have had hepatitis B virus infection in-creases the longer they engage in homosexual intercourse. Of men with over ten years of homosexuality, two-thirds or more have already had hepatitis B infection. Studies of Greek female prostitutes have shown that the longer they have been prosti-tutes, the likelier they are to have had hepatitis B infection, suggesting that women may also acquire hepatitis B infection sexually. There is less evidence that heterosexual men acquire this infection sexually.

It still isn't clear just why homosexual men and prostitutes have such a high risk of getting hepatitis B virus infection, but one clue was provided by the discovery that men who have the outer shell of the hepatitis B virus in their blood also have it in their semen. One recent study in London has shown that the practice of swallowing semen is related to the risk of hepa-titis B virus infection. If homosexual men swallow semen more often than heterosexual women, this could explain why homo-sexual men have this high risk. On the other hand, a study of homosexual men in New York suggested that those who engaged in passive anal intercourse had a greater risk of hepa-titis B virus infection than those who engaged only in other forms of homosexual behavior. This might mean that ejacula-tion of infected semen into the anal canal might be the way in which homosexual men transmit hepatitis B.

There is no effective treatment available for hepatitis B infection, but it is possible that hepatitis B will become the first sexually transmitted infection to be prevented by vaccination. Researchers at the National Institutes of Health and at Merck Sharpe and Dohme in the U.S., and in other countries as well, have been developing vaccines containing preparations of the outer shells of purified hepatitis B virus. These preparations have so far appeared to be free of the inner infectious virus and have protected chimpanzees from experimental inoculation with hepatitis B virus. In France, hepatitis B vaccine has already been given to hospital workers and patients who were exposed to other patients with hepatitis. None of the vaccinated people subsequently developed hepatitis B infection, while an unvaccinated group had a high rate of infection. It is likely that hepatitis B virus vaccines will eventually be judged safe for field testing in humans in the U.S., and it seems logical that male homosexuals and hospital workers would be among the prime beneficiaries of such a vaccine. Unfortunately, there is no immediate prospect for the control of any other sexually transmitted disease by vaccination.

SYPHILIS

During 1975 there were over 50,000 new cases of early syphilis (syphilis of less than one year's duration) reported in the U.S. Although the number of new cases of syphilis involving women has changed little in recent years, the annual number of new cases in men has nearly tripled in the U.S. since 1950. Over one-third of all new male cases of early syphilis in the U.S. during 1975 involved homosexual or bisexual men. In large coastal cities like London, New York, Los Angeles, San Francisco, Seattle, and Vancouver, the proportion is much greater. For example, in Seattle over two-thirds of all cases of early syphilis (including men and women) during the 1970s have involved homosexual or bisexual men.

The signs of syphilis usually make their first appearance two or three weeks after exposure to a contagious person. The disease is caused by a corkscrew-shaped bacterium, a spirochete named Treponema pallidum. (Some people claim to have acquired syphilis by contact with a door knob or toilet seat, but it is difficult to have sex with a door knob or a toilet seat. The couplet "Be careful on a toilet seat, the spirochete can jump six feet" is not well founded in fact.) The first sign of the primary stage is a small open sore, usually painless, on the genitals, mouth, or anus. This sore, the "chancre," lasts about two to six weeks, then heals by itself, even without treatment. But by this time, Treponema pallidum has entered the blood stream and has reached all parts of the body. If the disease is not diagnosed and treated, it may progress through two more stages. A few days or weeks after the chancre heals, a skin rash appears, heralding the onset of the secondary stage of syphilis. People are only contagious during the primary and secondary stages of syphilis, when the skin sores are teeming with infectious Treponema pallidum. Again, if treatment is not given, the rash eventually subsides and the infection enters a latent (silent) phase during which Treponema pallidum may or may not produce further damage.

The widely publicized Tuskegee study of black men with syphilis who were not given treatment, and an earlier study in Oslo, Norway, showed that one-third to one-half of all individuals who remain untreated after entering the latent phase go on to develop the tertiary stage of syphilis later in life. This involves damage to the heart and major blood vessels, brain, or other organs. The risk of developing these later complications is greater for men than women. This is of particular concern

for homosexual men since anal chancres usually go undetected, increasing the risk that homosexual men could enter
the latent phase without treatment. Blood tests performed on
homosexual men frequenting steam baths or gay bars have
shown that as many as 5 percent of them have unsuspected,
untreated syphilis. It seems clear that homosexual men who
have many sex partners should get routine periodic blood tests
for syphilis at least once a year. Treatment given during the
primary, secondary, or latent stages completely prevents
development of the tertiary complications.

Of special concern for women is the risk of transmitting
syphilis to the fetus during pregnancy. Proper treatment for
syphilis will prevent infection of the fetus during any future
pregnancy, but women who go untreated remain capable of
infecting the fetus for up to four years after catching syphilis
because the bacteria can circulate in the blood for up to four
years, even after the primary and secondary stages have subsided. For some reason, the fetus is safe during the first four
months of pregnancy, so that if the mother is blood tested
before four months and treated, the fetus will not be damaged
by syphilis. This is one of many reasons that pregnant women
should undergo their first prenatal examination during the
first three months of pregnancy.

When syphilis is suspected on the basis of symptoms or
exposure to an infected person, the diagnosis can be made in
two ways. The first is by examining fluid taken from an open
sore under a special microscope, known as a dark field microscope, which is generally available only in special venereal
disease clinics or in large hospital laboratories, but not in most
physicians' offices. The second way is by performing a blood
test. The blood tests take a few weeks to become positive, and
may not yet have become positive during the primary stage.
For this reason, individuals with genital sores need to be tested

both by dark field microscopy and by blood test to rule out syphilis.

AND NOW FOR SOMETHING REALLY DIFFER-ENT: CRABS AND GENITAL WARTS

Although national statistics of STD do not include crabs, Dr. Leslie Norins of Atlanta reported that sales of the number one over-the-counter lotion for treating lice (head or crab lice) increased 1200 percent from 1963 through 1974. Based on the total sales per 1,000 population, the 10 lousiest cities in the U.S. for 1974 and 1975 have been:

1. Providence, Rhode Island (Retained its number one ranking second year in a row)
2. Corpus Christi, Texas
3. Harrisburg, Pennsylvania
4. Albany-Troy, New York
5. Orlando, Florida
6. Boston, Massachusetts
7. Fresno, California
8. Eugene, Oregon
9. Manchester, New Hampshire
10. Las Vegas, Nevada

The problem has grown to the point that a national conference on lice and scabies was held at the University of Minnesota during 1976.

The most famous crab louse in the world is probably the one shown below, who answered to the name "Oh, shiiit," and began scuttling rapidly in the opposite direction shortly before he was impaled for microscopic photography for the Encyclopedia Britannica. When examined with the naked eye, he was only about the size of the head of a pin, pale tan in color, and he wiggled. His proper name is *Phthirus pubis*.

Ever wonder why crabs concentrate in the pubic area? One theory is that crabs like to have intercourse, just like the rest of us. To do it, the male and female crabs have to grasp adjoining hairs two millimeters apart, and the spacing of the hairs is just about right in the pubic area. Crabs cannot jump, and they cannot reach very far even when they stand on their tiptoes, so the only way to catch them is for your pubic hair to come within about two millimeters' distance from someone else's pubic hair or from where someone else's pubic hair has recently been. Crabs feed on your blood like a mosquito and they often stay in the same place for days. When the crabs' tummys are full, they do occasionally drop off into your underpants, sheets, or sleeping bag and curl up for a little nap. They seldom live longer than one day away from the body, but if you use a crab victim's clothing, bed, or sleeping bag within a day after he did, you could get screwed even without having intercourse. One interesting fact is that crabs seem to avoid dark-skinned people and prefer Caucasians.

Once a pair of crabs have set up housekeeping on you, it may take awhile before you notice it. The female crab louse lays about three eggs per day, up to a total of about thirty, each attached to a different pubic hair. These eggs are called nits, and each one takes about seven days to hatch. Each egg has a little lid on the top, and when they start popping open, a small but growing army of new crab lice move up to the front lines. A vague sensation becomes increasingly more localized, and people begin to take more notice of your behavior in public. One of the best clues is when your scratching becomes forceful enough to awaken you from sleep. However if you are unusually insensitive, this first assault wave may not reach the threshhold of your awareness, and it may take another three weeks before you notice something awry. It takes the young female crabs another two weeks after hatching to reach sexual maturity and start laying eggs, and another week for their eggs to start hatching.

The average time from exposure to diagnosis is about thirty days. Self-diagnosis is easy. You just have to catch one of the crabs, but two words of caution. First, after reading this description of crabs, it is normal to experience some pubic itching, but this should subside in a few hours and does not indicate you have crabs. Second, if you do think you have spotted a crab, you are not allowed to make a final self-diagnosis until you see him definitely wiggle or crawl. The majority of self-diagnosed crabs infections probably are not really crabs at all, but only crabophobia.

Since self-treatment is more common for crabs than for any other STD, and since crabs are probably as common as gonorrhea, we will offer some advice on therapy. After the diagnosis is firmly made, you should inspect other areas of the body, since crabs can also get into your eyebrows, eyelashes, and the hair under your arms or on your chest. The two forms of therapy used most often are gamma benzene (Kwell), a prescription lotion; or A-200 pyrinate, a lotion sold by pharmacies without a prescription. The effectiveness of these two remedies has not been compared. Instructions for application and for washing clothes, etc., are provided with these medications. Either lotion should be liberally applied to the entire pubic area and any other area that looks involved, but regardless of the instructions, we advise reapplying the lotion seven days after the original application. This is because the eggs are not affected by the lotion, and they take seven days to hatch. Simultaneous treatment of sex partners is necessary to prevent reinfection.

GENITAL WARTS

Warts that occur on the genitals are caused by a virus that is closely related but not identical to the virus which causes warts on the skin on other parts of the body. Two separate studies showed that about two-thirds of people who had sex with a person who had genital warts at the time of intercourse subsequently developed genital warts. The average time from sexual exposure until the appearance of genital warts was about three months in both studies. In one interesting study of fifteen English women who had been virgins before they had had intercourse with men who had warts on the penis, all fifteen developed warts on the vulva. During pregnancy, genital warts often enlarge rapidly, and then rapidly subside after delivery. Children born to women with genital warts occasionally develop a peculiar wart-like tumor involving the vocal cords and larynx.

Genital warts are usually treated by painting them with podophyllum, a dark resin obtained from certain plants in the United States or in the Himalayas. Some wart afficionados believe the Himalayan product is superior. Toxic reactions are common and this treatment should be undertaken only under medical supervision.

VAGINITIS: TRICHOMONAS, YEAST, AND NONSPECIFIC

A very small amount of white vaginal discharge occurs normally in all women. This discharge contains the vaginal cells which are constantly being shed and replaced by new cells, as are most other cells in the body (except for brain cells, which are never replaced and must last a lifetime).

An increased amount of clear mucous discharge is normal in women who are pregnant and during ovulation in many women's cycles. Symptoms of vaginitis include an abnormal vaginal discharge (increased amount, yellow or green color caused by pus cells); itching, irritation, redness, or swelling of the labia; or pain around the vaginal opening during intercourse. Burning may occur during urination either because the inflammation extends to the urethra or because the urine touches the inflamed labia. Abnormal vaginal odor is often attributed to vaginitis. The odor is produced by volatile substances which are manufactured by certain bacteria; and since many of these smellogenic bacteria do not actually produce inflammation, the term vaginitis is not correct.

The three common forms of vaginitis are called trichomonas vaginitis, yeast vaginitis, and nonspecific vaginitis. The vagina is normally acidic (vinegar is acidic, soap is basic). The vagina is usually neutral or basic with trichomonas infection, markedly acid with yeast infection, and variable with nonspecific vaginitis.

Trichomonas vaginitis is caused by a protozoan named Trichomonas vaginalis. It is more common than gonorrhea in women, and probably is the least well understood sexually transmitted organism. It rarely causes symptoms in men, and it is hard to find trichomonas in men, even in those who are sex partners of women with trichomonas infection. Nonetheless, we believe most male sex partners of infected women do carry the organism in their urethra.

There is a mystery about trichomonas infection in women that probably will be solved within the next decade. It concerns the fact that trichomonas causes no symptoms at all in some women; while in other women, trichomonas causes a bad-smelling vaginal discharge more profuse than that caused by any other infection. The trichomonas protozoan found in women with symptoms of vaginitis is much smaller in diameter than that found in women with no symptoms, but when the smaller forms of trichomonas are taken out of the vagina and grown in test tubes, they revert to larger forms. Thus, there seems to be some unknown factor in susceptible women that allows the smaller forms to grow and cause disease, whereas other women only allow the larger nondisease-producing forms to grow.

Since trichomonas is so common, it is fortunate that it does not seem to cause any serious complications other than vaginitis. It does not cause PID, for example. However, be cause it causes vaginitis, it does cause abnormal cervical Pap smears. About one-third of abnormal Pap smears are due to trichomonas infection. A Pap smear from a woman with trichomonas infection shows cervical cells plus pus cells from the vagina plus the trichomonas itself, so the diagnosis is often made unexpectedly by the technician reviewing the Pap smear. Some trichomonas infections can be missed by Pap smear, and a better way to make the diagnosis is to have the vaginal discharge examined under the microscope. The trichomonas swim along rapidly and are easily spotted.

Although trichomonas probably is usually spread sexually, it could be caught in other ways. For example, it is a very hardy organism and can live for several hours in water. One imaginative researcher in England noted that there are two basic kinds of water closets used in that country. One of them didn't splash when feces dropped into the bowl, but the other splashed to a height well above the rim of the bowl—high enough to wet the unsuspecting vagina with a thin film of tri-chomonas if any happened to be lurking in the toilet waiting to pounce. The risk of splashing is greater for squatters than for sitters, since the distance the feces fall is the main factor which determines whether there will be a splash. The possibil-ity of this type of nonsexual infection is suggested by the fact that Trichomonas vaginalis occurs in post-menopausal women more often than any other STD. The British suggest a good way to prevent getting trichomonas this way: flush the public toilet before you sit down to get rid of any that might be lurking in the water.

Yeast vaginitis is caused by a fungus, usually by one called Candida albicans. Vaginal yeast infection is very common but is not usually sexually transmitted. Yeast is normally present in small amounts in the vagina of about 30 percent of women, and yeast normally inhabits the mouth and intestinal tract of many men and women. It causes vaginitis only when it over-grows the other microorganisms in the vagina. This overgrowth often happens during pregnancy, or in women with diabetes. There is also good evidence that women taking birth control pills are especially susceptible to vaginal yeast infection. Some-times the infection keeps recurring after every course of treat-ment until the oral contraceptives are stopped.

Antibiotics taken for some unrelated problem, such as for acne, also commonly cause yeast vaginitis by killing off the normal bacteria of the vagina and allowing yeast to move in and set up housekeeping. Yeast infection does not cause a profuse, bad-smelling vaginal discharge like that of trichomonas; instead the yeast produces scanty white clumps of discharge which resemble cottage cheese. This is associated with severe itching of the vulva, often with irritation, redness, and swelling of the labia minora. Yeast infection can be sexually transmitted and can cause a similar itching, red rash on the penis—most often beneath the foreskin of uncircumcised men. Infected men can, in turn, pass the infection on to women.

Nonspecific vaginitis is not included among the top ten sexually transmitted diseases only because we do not know what proportion of cases are sexually transmitted. Neither its cause nor a satisfactory treatment are known. Nevertheless, it is extremely common, and its symptoms resemble those of other sexually transmitted diseases. Symptoms of vaginitis are usually attributed to nonspecific vaginitis if trichomonas, yeast, gonorrhea, or herpes cannot be found when the vagina and cervix are examined. Most cases are probably caused by bacteria. Although the specific microbial cause is uncertain, there is suspicion that a bacteria named Hemophilus vaginalis is the cause of some cases.

Nonspecific vaginitis can result when a couple has vaginal intercourse immediately after rectal intercourse, because feces are bad for the vagina. Rectal bacteria are particularly likely to cause vaginal malodor. Some cases seem related to the use of a tampon during menstruation, particularly if the tampon is left in the vagina for prolonged periods. Direct irritation or allergic reactions can cause nonspecific vaginitis in the absence of any infection, and these reactions can be caused by vaginal spermicidal preparations, feminine hygiene sprays, douching, or even by the antibiotic-containing ointments used to treat nonspecific vaginitis itself.

A FEW WORDS ABOUT THE OTHER
LEADING CONTENDERS

Infectious mononucleosis, as discussed above, is probably spread by swapping saliva with someone, since the causative agent, herpes EB virus, can be found in the saliva for prolonged periods in individuals who have had infectious mono. However, transmission by sexual intercourse has not been ruled out. A Navy study showed that men who previously had infectious mono were much more likely to get gonorrhea during a cruise than men who had never had infectious mono. This suggests that the same sort of behavior which previously led to mono subsequently led to gonorrhea. Of course it could be that men who do a lot of kissing also have a lot of sexual intercourse.

Scabies is caused by a small burrowing insect—a mite—named Sarcoptes scabiei. It is highly contagious among children as well as among sexually active adults, and for some reason it seems to have occurred in epidemic waves in the U.S. about every fifteen years. The tiny mite burrows into the skin, typically in the webs between the fingers, around the beltline, and around the nipples, genitals, and the lower buttocks. Small red bumps and short burrows under the skin develop intense itching. The treatment is the same as that used for crabs.

Chancroid is an ulcer which resembles syphilis (hence the name, which means chancre-like), but unlike the painless syphilis chancre, chancroid is painful. It is more common in uncircumcised men than in circumcised men but is rare in the U.S. Granuloma inguinale is too rare and too unpleasant to describe further here. Both chancroid and granuloma inguinale are now easily treatable.

Genital molluscum contagiosum is a virus infection which

causes small, waxy, salmon-colored bumps on the skin which may last for several months before they go away but do no permanent harm. This infection is more common among children, who develop nongenital forms of the infection. Dermatologists know how to scrape them away for rapid cosmetic improvement.

Rounding out the list of the ten leading contenders are three diseases which recent evidence suggests are sexually transmitted among homosexual men. Shigella dysentery, amebic dysentery, and giardiasis are all extremely important causes of disease in those undeveloped countries where food and drinking water become contaminated with feces. In the U.S., these diseases are relatively uncommon in the general population, but there is evidence that homosexual men frequently acquire them sexually. The organisms which cause these diseases live in the intestinal tract and are shed in the feces. Homosexual men probably acquire these infections by "rimming" (analingus) or by fellating a male who has recently had rectal intercourse with a third party who was carrying one of these intestinal organisms.

IMPROVING THE ODDS:
TEN WAYS TO PREVENT STD

Prevention is really a matter of cutting risks, so first let us define the risks. Most of the available information deals with gonorrhea. In one fascinating unpublished study done many years ago, ninety-five men had intercourse one time with women known to have gonorrhea, and only five of the ninety-five caught gonorrhea. This is the lowest estimate of risk. Two more recent studies of Navy men showed that the calculated risk of catching gonorrhea from infected prostitutes was about 25 to 35 percent. Interestingly, the risk went up for repeated acts of intercourse, so that about 75 percent of men who had intercourse five or six times with an infected prostitute developed gonorrhea. Thus, one way for a man to cut the risk of getting gonorrhea is to settle for once or twice—an approach that becomes more appealing the older you get. The risk of a woman becoming infected after exposure to a man with gonorrhea has not been studied. Oddly, the risk of having gonorrhea seems to be higher for women who are blood group B than for those who are blood group O or A, so if you happen to be blood group B, you should be especially careful about gonorrhea.

The risk of men catching chlamydia from infected women is not known, but in one study about 40 percent of women exposed to men with chlamydia-NGU were found to have chlamydia infection of the cervix.

Figures for the risk of catching syphilis vary, depending on whose statistics you read. Just to give a ballpark estimate, the risk after one or more exposures to someone with primary or secondary syphilis is probably greater than 30 percent and less than 85 percent. For genital herpes, a wild guess is that at least a third of people exposed to someone with open genital herpes sores will catch herpes. The risk of sexual transmission of CMV, ureaplasma, hepatitis B, and crabs is not known.

There are ten frequently recommended ways to prevent STD, three of which work pretty well. One textbook for high school sex education teachers suggests students be taught the following ways for preventing venereal disease: abstinence; monogamy; selectivity in choosing a partner; asking your partner if he or she has VD; douching; washing with soap and water; using a condom; using a diaphragm or vaginal spermicide; urination after intercourse; and medical prevention (e.g. antibiotics). Abstinence from sex works well to prevent STD, but abstinence is not what this book is about. Having relations with only one person at a time ("serial monogamy") is a very good way to avoid STD. However, many people keep looking until they find someone they want to live with. And there is no guarantee your sex partner is monogamous, even if you are.

One variation on the theme of abstinence which should be more widely publicized is something we call "temporary post-exposure abstinence." Suppose you are married but you have just taken a trip and had sex with someone you met on the trip who you probably won't ever see again. How long should you wait for symptoms of STD to develop after sex with the casual partner before you resume sex with your spouse without fear of infecting him or her? The most practical advice is to wait about a week, since signs of gonorrhea and herpes usually appear within seven days after exposure. Unfortunately NGU, syphilis, and crabs take longer and you would have to wait about six weeks to be reasonably sure you hadn't picked up any of these. You would have to wait even longer to exclude venereal warts and hepatitis B, and it has been our experience that altruism starts giving way to lust after about a week of abstinence in most cases. If you are a woman, signs of gonorrhea may be harder to detect during the first week after exposure, so the system of temporary abstinence for one week after a high risk exposure isn't foolproof, but it certainly could reduce the risk of spreading gonorrhea and genital herpes.

What about selectivity in choosing sex partners? "Promiscuous" is defined as "indiscriminate in one's choice of sex partners," but the word is usually used to mean one has "too many" sex partners, a use that perpetuates judgmental and moralistic attitudes about sexual behavior. This was illustrated at a meeting on STD held during 1975 in England, where the word was used twenty-nine times during the conference in reference to women and not once to men.

Anyone can be carry STD. Nevertheless, some generalizations about STD carriers are hard to avoid. For women, the risk of catching STD is lowest for sex with another woman, intermediate for sex with a heterosexual man, and highest for sex with a bisexual man. For men, the risk is obviously highest for those who have sex with a female prostitute or highest for those who have sex with a female prostitute or with another man. For both sexes the risk is highest for intercourse with casual new acquaintances, particularly those whose life style brings them into frequent contact with STD, or whose access to acceptable health care is so limited or whose social or emotional problems are so overwhelming that they do not obtain treatment promptly for STD when it occurs.

To swallow or not to swallow—that is the question. Selectivity in sexual practices can also be considered. For example, those faced with the difficult decision of whether or not to swallow the semen during fellatio should remember that the caloric content of semen does not even begin to approach its microbial content.

The idea of asking a prospective sex partner if he or she has STD is hard to carry out, although any opportunity to turn the conversation around to genital herpes should, of course, be seized upon. The idea of actually looking for evidence of STD has been widely publicized as "the call-girl ritual." A more general term might be "exploratory foreplay." Prostitutes examine the penis of prospective customers for evidence of sores or warts and check for the presence of gonorrhea or NGU by milking the penis from back to front to press out any discharge from the urethra. Some clear secretions may normally form in the urethra during sexual arousal, but the presence of white or yellow discharge is a sign of gonorrhea or NGU. The problem with inspecting the merchandise is that the aphorism, "What you see is what you get," does not always apply to STD. For example, trichomonas, the gonococcus,

CMV, hepatitis B virus, and ureaplasma are probably most often spread by men and women who have no symptoms. For homosexual men, it is said that 95 percent of anal syphilis chancres can be seen with the naked eye if the buttocks are spread apart. Men are even less likely to be able to detect signs of STD by touch, sight, or smell in their female sex partner.

It generally takes more than 60,000,000 sperm deposited in the vagina to cause a single pregnancy, and it probably takes more than a few microorganisms deposited in the vagina or urethra to start up most new genital infections. In theory, anything that lowers the number of organisms deposited—for example, douching by the female or urinating by the male promptly after intercourse—may lower the risk of infection. Unfortunately, there is no evidence to prove that douching, washing, or urinating after intercourse prevents STD. In fact, one study involving Navy men showed that those who washed and/or urinated soon after intercourse had the same risk of gonorrhea as those who did not.

Another way of possibly lowering the number of micro-organisms ejaculated into (or transferred from) the vagina is by using intravaginal spermicidal foams, creams, or gels which not only kill sperm, but also kill a variety of STD microorganisms including the gonococcus and spirochete—at least in the test tube. Studies recently conducted at the University of Pittsburgh seemed to show that women who use Conceptrol Cream before intercourse in the same way as directed for use for contraception were significantly protected from gonorrhea. If these findings can be confirmed, this would mean that a woman who elects to use a diaphragm plus a spermicidal medication for contraception is also protecting herself against gonorrhea (and possibly against other forms of STD). Some sexually active people who are highly motivated to prevent STD, clubs of swinging couples, for example, object to the use of intravaginal medication for prevention of venereal disease because the flavors do not enhance oral sex. This is not necessarily an insurmountable technological problem in the space age.

Moving along to preventive methods which are more effective but less popular, the condom is undoubtedly effective for reducing the risk of all of the top ten STDs except for crabs. A campaign in Sweden which increased sales of condoms from ten million per year to thirty million per year was accompanied by a sharp drop in gonorrhea rates. Unfortunately, it is hard to convince any man who ever used one that condoms are not a hassle or that they do not reduce the tactile sensation on the penis during intercourse. Despite the hassle, the condom is still the ideal method of STD prophylactic for that particular group of men or women whose personal situations dictate that they do everything possible to minimize the risk of STD (the married person at a convention, for example, who has intercourse with a casual contact or prostitute and does not want to bring home to the spouse anything more exciting than Fralinger's original salt water taffy).

"Medical prophylaxis" means medical treatment before or after exposure. Some diseases such as herpes, CMV, hepatitis B, and genital warts are caused by viruses for which no known antibiotic treatment or prophylaxis exists. Several studies suggest that injections of gamma globulin given soon after exposure (usually available through public health departments) are of benefit in preventing hepatitis B in people exposed to contaminated blood, either accidentally or by blood transfusion. We do not know whether gamma globulin would reduce the risk of sexual transmission of hepatitis B virus.

It has recently been shown that prophylactic treatment

with a long-acting tetracycline medication reduces the risk of catching NGU and gonorrhea. When two of the tetracycline pills were given by mouth soon after exposure or as "morning after pills" to sailors who had sex with prostitutes, the risk of catching NGU was reduced by 85 percent. The risk of these sailors catching gonorrhea was also reduced by about half, but gonorrhea caused by strains of gonococci which were relatively resistant to tetracycline and other antibiotics, was not prevented.

Therefore, there is a proper reluctance to encourage people to use tetracycline after casual sexual encounters for fear that tetracycline-resistant strains of gonococci would eventually come to predominate. The low doses of tetracycline used by hundreds of thousands of young people in the U.S. for acne would not be very effective for prevention or treatment of gonorrhea, and antibiotic treatment should not be undertaken without medical advice. Routine prophylactic treatment with ampicillin or other penicillin antibiotics that you might have lying around the house is definitely not advisable, since the risk of an allergic reaction to the penicillin antibiotics (even for people who have taken them previously without side effects) exceeds the risk of catching STD.

Finally, as mentioned earlier, a vaccine for hepatitis B virus infection is hoped for soon. Research is going on to develop vaccines for gonorrhea, syphilis, herpes virus, and CMV, but there seems to be no prospect for vaccines for these diseases in the near future.

To sum up the protections against sexually transmitted diseases, the risk of getting STD can definitely be reduced by use of a condom, by taking a tetracycline after intercourse, or by abstinence from sexual intercourse. The risk of getting gonorrhea in women appears to be reduced by the use of an intravaginal spermicidal preparation just before intercourse.

Careful selection of your sex partner and sex practice, and "exploratory foreplay" probably could prevent some cases of STD. Douching (don't douche if you use a diaphragm or foam), washing, and urinating by the male after intercourse may or may not reduce the risk of STD enough to make the use of these methods worth the trouble.

IF PREVENTION DID NOT WORK

Medical students learn that the physician who attempts to treat himself has a fool for a doctor. The same applies to anyone who tries self-treatment. Unfortunately, the quality of diagnosis and treatment available for anyone with STD in the U.S. is so spotty that one needs to know not only how to recognize the symptoms of STD, but also how to find some-one reasonably likely to be able to diagnose and treat those particular symptoms.

For example, most physicians in private practice do not have the necessary equipment to do a microscopic exami-nation for syphilis, and some do not even perform culture or Gram stain examination for suspected gonorrhea. On the other hand, a woman with symptoms of vaginal discharge would be wasting her time going to the public venereal disease clinic in some cities where the clinics test for nothing but gonorrhea and syphilis and make no attempt to diagnose or treat the other sexually transmitted diseases which cause vaginal discharge.

To find out what services are offered free by your local health department, look in the phone book under the city or county government health department listings for a venereal disease clinic phone number, and call that number. Some health departments camouflage the VD clinic by giving it another name, like Adult Health Clinic or Social Hygiene Clinic. If you can't find the right listing, then just call any health department number and ask for the VD clinic number. Alternatively, there is a national VD help line in Philadelphia which can be called toll free at any time, day or night. The number is I-800-523-I885. This national service is called OPERATION VENUS—VD INFORMATION, and will answer informational questions, send free information in the mail, and will also give you the name and number of a local private physician or public clinic that will treat STD at low cost or free.

There are four important signs of sexually transmitted diseases: abnormal vaginal discharge, discharge from the penis, genital sores, and lower abdominal pain in women. A vaginal discharge which is yellow or green, has a bad odor. or is associated with irritation or itching of the vulva, with pain during intercourse, or with lower abdominal pain is usually abnormal and indicates vaginitis, cervicitis (inflammation of the cervix), or PID. The commonest causes of these symptoms are yeast, trichomonas, gonorrhea, and nonspecific vaginitis. If the main symptom is itching of the vulva, the diagnosis is probably yeast vaginitis. Vaginal yeast infection also causes a scanty, white discharge which resembles curds of cottage cheese. In contrast, Trichomonas vaginitis causes a profuse bad-smelling discharge, usually with less itching.

With any of these symptoms, a woman in the U.S. would do best to consult a women's health care specialist, a gynecologist for example, rather than a public venereal disease clinic, unless she knows that the STD clinic is enlightened enough to be in the business of treating all causes of vaginitis. The tests that should be performed to find the cause of vaginal discharge include examination of the discharge under a microscope (a "wet mount" test) to detect trichomonas or yeast, and a culture test for gonorrhea. If all of these tests are negative, the diagnosis is usually "nonspecific vaginitis" (which means no one knows what is wrong).

Trichomonas vaginitis is treated with a prescription drug called metronidazole (Flagyl) which is taken by mouth. Adults should take 500 mg every twelve hours for five days. This dose cures over 95 percent of infections. A single dose of two grams is becoming more widely used because it is effective and convenient. Flagyl may cause birth defects in experimental animals, and although there is no evidence it causes similar problems in humans, it should not be taken during early pregnancy. Pregnant women are usually given Flagyl in the form of suppositories inserted into the vagina. This relieves symptoms but is not very effective for long term cure. The male sex partner(s) should also take Flagyl at the same time as the woman with trichomonas vaginitis, since the male carries the trichomonas in his urethra without having any symptoms and he will just reinfect the woman if he is not treated. Alcoholic beverages should be avoided while Flagyl is being taken because alcohol causes severe stomach upset when taken with Flagyl. Occasionally, Flagyl causes the white blood cell count to drop. One disturbing finding is that in very high doses, Flagyl causes lung cancer in mice. It does not cause cancer in other experimental animals, and the U.S. Food and Drug Administration recently concluded that the available evidence does not suggest Flagyl causes cancer in humans.

Vaginal yeast infections are usually treated with one of three drugs (either mycostatin, miconazole, or clotrimazole) which are placed into the vagina once or twice a day for two weeks. The question often comes up as to whether the male sex partner should be simultaneously treated. If he has a rash on his penis, he should get a prescription of his own. Otherwise, as soon as the woman feels up to it, he can have sex with her each day after she places her medication into her vagina. Then he will be treated, too. It is probably not a good idea to use intravaginal spermicides at the same time as intravaginal antibiotics are used, so women using these forms of contraception should avoid intercourse until treatment is completed.

No one knows how to treat nonspecific vaginitis. Research in progress now should lead to better knowledge about its cause and treatment within the next year or two.

A second sign of sexually transmitted disease is discharge from the man's penis or burning on urination. In young men, these symptoms usually represent urethritis, either gonorrhea or non-gonococcal urethritis (NGU). If the discharge is green or yellow and it started less than a week after the time of exposure, the chances are it is gonorrhea. If it is white or clear and appeared more than a week after the time of exposure, it is probably NGU, but the only way to find out is to get it checked. For this condition, the best place to get taken care of is generally a public STD or VD clinic since the main thing these clinics do in the U.S. is take care of urethritis and they do it free. The discharge is tested by collecting it on a cotton swab and smearing it onto a glass microscope slide for examination under the microscope. This smear test can be done immediately and the diagnosis is available within minutes. Many physicians in private practice do not own a microscope, and unless they practice in a large clinic with a laboratory nearby, they cannot do this simple test.

The public clinics will want to know your name and address (you can always make up a name and address if you do not want to have your name on record in a VD clinic) and, if you turn out to have gonorrhea, they will want to know who your sex partners are. They will ask you to inform your partner and they will offer to do it if you do not want to. Whether or not you tell the name of your partner is up to you, but remember, your sex partner almost certainly is not aware of having gonorrhea, so you have the responsibility to tell him or her or them or to have someone else do it.

If the sex partner remains uninformed, three things will happen. If the two of you have sex again, you will be reinfected. If the sex partner remains untreated, there is a good chance that a serious complication of gonorrhea will develop, particularly if the partner is a woman. It is often difficult to inform one's sex partner about having STD, because not everyone feels comfortable with a preamble such as, "By the way, there is something I have not told you about yet . . ." This is usually not because having STD is regarded as bad, but because some relationships that become complicated by STD are dishonest. One of the few advantages of having STD is the opportunity for converting a dishonest relationship into an open one.

Genital sores are a third symptom of sexually transmitted diseases. These are potentially serious. One study in Columbus, Ohio, showed that of one hundred men with open sores on the penis, about half had syphilis or herpes and the other half had cuts or abrasions of the skin or sores of unknown causes. Syphilitic ulcers are usually painless and appear two or three weeks after exposure, whereas herpes ulcers are usually painful, begin as blisters, and appear just a few days after exposure. But exceptions occur, and when any open ulcer appears on the penis or vulva, it must be examined for both syphilis and herpes.

Most physicians make a diagnosis of genital herpes infection on the basis of the appearances of the lesions alone. Although the virus can be grown from the vesicle, pustule or ulcer, this is expensive and not generally available. The diagnosis can often be proved simply by performing a Pap smear on one of the sores. This is the same test used to detect cancer of the cervix but it can also be used to test for herpes virus instead of cancer. When herpes virus is present the Pap smear shows clumps of herpes virus within the cells or other changes characteristic of herpes virus infection.

As of August, 1976, no treatment is known to be effective for reducing the severity of an individual attack of genital herpes or for preventing relapses, but some physicians are willing to offer unproven methods of treatment to patients who insist on it. The severity of each episode and the frequency of recurrences are highly variable, even in an individual. People who experience a severe initial episode and then use some quack remedy during the later milder recurrences are easily convinced that the treatment is working, but they are only observing the natural history of the disease.

One commonly used treatment involves application of a colored dye (neutral red or proflavine) to each of the individual lesions, followed by exposure of the dyed lesions to fluorescent light. This treatment, called "light-dye" or "photoinactivation" treatment, has been shown to have no effect on genital herpes in three recent controlled studies in the U.S. and England. Although the light-dye treatment does kill herpes virus in test tubes, there is some evidence this treatment also alters some of the virus particles, causing them to make the cells in which they are growing undergo malignant change, transforming them into cancer cells. This raises the possibility that the light-dye treatment not only does not work, but may conceivably increase the risk of cancer caused by herpes virus.

Possible methods for preventing recurrent herpes include vaccines and methods for increasing the general level of resistance to viral infections. Two herpes virus vaccines are commercially available in Europe. They cannot be sold in the United States because there is no evidence that they work, and it is theoretically possible that they could cause cancer. Smallpox vaccine was once used in attempts to prevent recurrent herpes, even though smallpox and herpes are unrelated viruses. There is no theoretical reason why smallpox vaccine should work, and one controlled study showed smallpox vaccine has no effect in preventing recurrences. Other more promising forms of treatment and several possible methods for preventing recurrences of herpes are currently being studied. Until some form of treatment or prevention has actually been shown to work, once the diagnosis of genital herpes is made, it is a waste of money and possibly dangerous to accept treatment.

LOWER ABDOMINAL PAIN IN WOMEN

There are dozens of causes of lower abdominal or pelvic pain in women, but one of the most common is pelvic inflammatory disease (PID). The signs of PID and how not to have it taken care of can be illustrated best by a case history from the annals of bad medicine.

Gayle T. is a twenty-two-year-old woman who came to a hospital emergency room one night because of crampy lower abdominal pain. The pain had begun a week earlier during her menstrual period, but it persisted after the period ended and became more severe than the cramps she had usually experienced with menstruation. She had also noticed a recent increase in vaginal discharge, and she was using an IUD for contraception.

The gynecology intern who examined her in the emergency room recognized this as a typical case of PID, but he left the IUD in place. He performed a culture test for gonorrhea, gave her some medication for pain and a prescription for tetracycline tablets, and told her to phone back for the results of her gonorrhea culture test. The pain medication relieved the cramps for several days, so Gayle did not fill the prescription and did not phone in to get the results of her culture.

After about ten days, her pain worsened again, and the hospital phoned to inform her that her gonorrhea culture was positive. An examination by a resident now showed she had developed definite swelling of both uterine tubes. The likelihood of her being permanently sterilized by the infection had increased from about 5 percent to over 25 percent. She was treated with an injection to make sure at least some antibiotic got into her, was given some free tetracycline to continue taking at home, and the IUD was removed.

She had entered into a new sexual relationship with a man three weeks before her first symptoms of PID began and she continued to have sex with him and with her old boyfriend as well, but no attempt was made to examine either sex partner. A month later, Gayle returned with a second episode of gonococcal PID. This time both of her sex partners were persuaded to come in for examination. It took a great deal of coaxing because both men were sure they were not infected since they had no symptoms (It is about ten times as hard to get a man to come in for a STD check as it is to convince a woman. This seems to be partly because it is not well enough publicized that men can have STD without symptoms, and partly because it threatens the male's machismo to admit he might be the one carrying STD.) Gayle's new partner turned out to have nonsymptomatic gonorrhea (he was a chronic carrier and probably had given it to Gayle twice), and her boyfriend admitted to having developed symptoms of gonorrhea and going to the health department for treatment about the same time Gayle developed her first episode of PID (Gayle probably gave him his infection).

This episode illustrates some of the mistakes which allow

PID to cause infertility. Gayle waited too long to have her symptoms checked. Symptoms of lower abdominal pain may represent PID and should not be ignored, especially if the symptoms are associated with abnormal vaginal discharge, with IUD use, or fever. Abdominal pain caused by PID often begins during menstruation but is more severe than that caused by menstrual cramps. In Gayle's case, the IUD was not removed promptly at the first visit. (At one time it was thought the IUD could be left in place if antibiotics were given, but gynecologists are increasingly removing IUDs and giving antibiotics as soon as signs of PID occur.) Gayle was seen by a physician she did not know, who failed to communicate to her the importance of her condition, to obtain her confidence, or to perceive her unwillingness to carry out the prescription. Failure to examine her male sex partner resulted in her reinfection and further damage to her uterine tubes.

The best physician for a woman to consult for suspected PID is still a gynecologist—ideally, the one advising her on contraception—who will take time to help her understand what is going on and will continue to see her during and after treatment to deal with the questions of possible change in contraceptive method, infertility, and residual pain.

One major problem with consulting a gynecologist is that gynecologists still sign an agreement not to take male patients before they can be certified as gynecologists. This seems like a head-in-the-sand attitude since such a large part of gynecology involves sexually transmitted genital infections. At any rate, it often means that steps to arrange examination and treatment of her male sex partner need to be initiated by the woman. The male sex partner should go to a VD clinic, not to a physician in private practice. Many physicians remain unaware that men can have gonorrhea without symptoms, and will not perform culture tests for gonorrhea or offer treatment if symptoms are absent.

The kind of thing that happened to Gayle happens again and again. The patient, his or her sex partner, and the physician fail to communicate, and the result is mutual distrust. All of these relationships are important to us as are our relationships to our contraceptives and the microbes we share. Information, understanding, and communication can help to keep these intricate relationships healthy and useful.

IF HE CAN DO IT,
I CAN DO IT